The Book
of
End-Time Fire

by Christine Beadsworth

All Scriptures used are from the Amplified, KJV or MKJV Bible.

ISBN number 978-0-359-25435-4

Copyright: Fresh Oil Releases 2019

First Edition

First Printing

Fresh Oil Releases

41 Tharina Road

Somerset West

South Africa 7130

Further articles can be found at:

https://freshoilreleases.wordpress.com/

Podcasts are available at:

https://www.podomatic.com/podcasts/freshairreleases

or 'Fresh Air Releases' on Soundcloud

The author may be reached at freshoilreleases@polka.co.za

Dedication

**To all those who have been willing to pay the price
to become part of the Company of the Burning Ones,
the sealed carriers of His jealous, fiery love
as He cleanses His threshing floor.**

Son 8:6 Set me like a seal upon your heart,
like a seal upon your arm;
for love is as strong as death,
jealousy is as hard and cruel as Sheol .
Its flashes are flashes of fire,
a most vehement flame [*the very flame of the Lord*]!

Contents

Introduction

On 22nd December 2010, I became acutely aware of the smell of smoke and burning in the passageway of my home. I searched to find its source and upon finding nothing, I even packed an overnight bag, in case there were wires burning in the roof area and I would be forced to flee in the middle of the night.

The next morning, the lord woke me with a phrase, "Spirit of Judgment and Burning" and I knew that what I had smelled the night before had been a spiritual odor rather than a natural one. God was making an announcement that a visitation for my household had been appointed by Heaven. Exactly 4 days later, my whole personal world turned upside down as my husband walked out with no explanation. It took many days and floods of tears and agonized prayer, before I began to understand that all that was happening to me was a personal experience of what occurs when the Spirit of Judgment and Burning enters the lives of His children. My husband did return to me 4 years later but how could I write about the spirit of judgment and burning if I had never experienced it? He had come to bring cleansing and separation from all that would mar His testimony within His Beloved. He would be working in both my husband and I, but we stood before Him, not as one unit, but as individual vessels.

Pro 16:2   All the ways of a man are pure in his own eyes, but the Lord weighs the spirits (the thoughts and intents of the heart).

He had come to divide between soul and spirit, between bone and marrow - and the heat of this encounter with the Spirit of Judgment and Burning would bring all dross to the surface; it's intent to purify and purge and beautify.

He had come to make me a weapon fit for His purpose. And I needed to surrender to His superior wisdom and, more than that, cooperate with what He intended to do in this fiery furnace.

Isa 4:3 And it shall be, he who is left in Zion, and he who remains in Jerusalem, shall be called holy, even everyone who is written among the living in Jerusalem; Isa 4:4 when the Lord shall have washed away the filth of the daughters of Zion, and shall have purged the blood of Jerusalem from its midst by the spirit of judgment, and by the spirit of burning.

His Word unfailingly comforted me during the many days of visitation. The fact that I smelled the smoke in the passageway was a prophetic sign, as the Lord was indicating there would be a passage of time when this visitation would take place and then be removed. There would be an afterward... There was Divine reason and specific purpose behind each detail of this tailor-made Refiner's fire. I wanted to be called 'Holy', set apart for Kingdom purposes. I wanted His will, even though the process of bringing it forth was most painful to my flesh. Yet there was not one flame that touched my world that was not accompanied by a powerful sense of His nearness and comfort. And I knew that many others all over the world were facing their own furnace visitations. He connected me with handpicked precious saints who could share notes, bring words of wisdom and direction and, most of all, just provide kind, gentle company while the flames raged relentlessly. And oh, the jewels of revelation that came to light in this place!

I have learned to love the Refiner's fire and the incredible kindness of the Lord in leading me, the daughter He loves to repentance by telling me my faults. I understand He is preparing me to share His glory and the only way I will ever even be apportioned the honour of carrying a minute measure of His glory, is if I truly grasp that without Him, I am nothing; that unless He gives me words to write, I have nothing of value to say; that the robe of righteousness my Bridegroom bought for me is the most valuable garment I will ever possess! It is vastly superior to any tailor-made couture garment that the Harlot Church of Babylon could ever conjure up for me; for without it's ruby fold's enveloping my frail earthen vessel, I will never see Him face to face or be able to enter the full glory of His manifest presence.

I know that all who have desired to know Him more deeply as I have, have also been through a long season in the Refiner's fire. He prepares His weapons of war with meticulous precision. As He describes in Isaiah 54:16, He creates the smith that blows upon the coals and brings forth a weapon fit for its purpose. He crafts individual situations in their minute detail in order to have maximum impact upon each particular weapon He is forming. Has our Beloved Lord left us in this season? No! No-one can snatch us out of His hand. And yes, the enemy has been allowed to attack, but in God's divine wisdom, he only becomes the 'smith' working to bring forth God's will and his services are removed when his usefulness is over. Not one blow too many is allowed to fall.

I know I probably don't have to tell you this, but the season of the Spirit of Judgment and Burning which has tested the mettle of His forerunners has dragged on so very much longer than expected. Years have ticked by and if you, like me, have finally given up struggling against the blows that are intended to forge the weapon, you have found yourself coming to a strange place of peace and trust; a place of lying still in the Divine Forger's appointed place of shaping, trusting His timing and finally being secure in the wisdom of His choice of 'smith' or agent. Just like David, who fought a lion and a bear far from the public eye, we too are being trained to bring down 'Goliath' and step into the Father's ordained place of kingdom influence.

In fact, after the 'smith' has done its work, we are brought to a place of hardly noticing that the flames are dying down and that we are finally being removed from the blast of the furnace. Perhaps it is because we have become so aware of the intimate touch of His hand as our Father polishes His weapons of war until He can see His face in them, that all else 'grows strangely dim in the light of His glory and grace'... It is a good place to be; a place of having entered His rest, of ceasing from all striving to save oneself from suffering. And all the while, there is an angel recording the measure of suffering we have endured - for we are appointed to share His glory in proportion to the extent we have been subjected to suffering. We are appointed to reign in a metron of rule connected to the measure of affliction in the preparatory chapter. But more on this wonderful truth in later chapters...

You see, God is preparing an army that He will use to wage war upon another army; that of the dark one who covets the throne of God. And this vast company of warriors of light must be put through their paces and fully trained BEFORE the thick of the real end-time battles. The sons of Zion are about to be pitted against the sons of Greece.

Zec 9:13 For I have bent Judah for me as a bow; I filled it with Ephraim, and I will stir up your sons, O Zion, against your sons, O Greece, and make you as the sword of a mighty man.

You are stronger than you realise after all you have been through. You just don't realise it because you are tired from the years of preparation. But you have been shaped with precise detail for specific assignments that Heaven's Battle Headquarters knows are ahead of you. And Christ in you is equal to the task. The things that made you break down in fear and trembling years ago no longer even cause you to flinch. There is steel down in your soul. You have become a weapon ready for the Masters' use. He is coming to bring judgment on Babylon using His weapons of war:

Jer 51:19 The portion of Jacob is not like them; for He is the former of all things: and Israel is the rod of his inheritance: the LORD of hosts is his name. Jer 51:20 You are my battle axe and weapons of war: for with you will I break in pieces the nations, and with you will I destroy kingdoms;

The judgments decreed by Jeremiah upon the physical nation of Babylon for its sin against Zion in Jer 51 will now be meted out upon the spiritual Babylon; the woman who is drunk with the blood of the saints as Rev 17:5,6 describes. It is executed using God's battle axe and weapons of war.

Some years ago, I was shown from the Book of Zechariah chapter 3 onwards that there are 5 stages of release and setting in place for His remnant. You may identify with any one of these stages, as some forerunners are a few steps ahead of others:

1. First, there is a removal from the fire of those who have been purified. This signifies the former season of preparation has ended.

2. Then there is a removal of the dirty, stained garments of a past refining season and the release of new rich garments, garments of state (Zech 3:4).

3. Then there is a decree issued from the throne assigning us an appointed place to stand before the throne (Zech 3:7, Rev 3:12).

4. Fourthly, there is a release of a continual supply of oil to those who make up this Branch Company, speaking of the anointing and equipping by the seven Spirits of God, described in chapter 4 of Zechariah.

5. Lastly, there is a crowning and release of the Melchizedek priesthood, the corporate Branch, depicted from Zechariah 6:9 onwards. This is accompanied by the baptism of fire, or the lighting of the two menorahs which have been filled to the brim with a continuous supply of oil. This lighting is accomplished by lighting the central shamash candle first and then using this flame to light all other branches of this corporate double Menorah Company.

So let us start by recapping on the work of the Refiner's fire in the next chapter. The forerunner company goes through this ahead of the rest of the Body, in order to make them fire-proof vessels carrying a fiery anointing during the day that burns like an oven.

1. Forged in the Refiners Fire

I have a friend who is a Jeweler and I asked her to explain to me just exactly what happens in the process of dealing with dross, and she said to me: the metal, silver, for instance, is in the crucible and heat is applied from underneath. Now, silver, is chemically bonded to dross, so the initial fire brings the dross to the surface so that you can see it and this is what happens when God initially applies the Refiner's Fire to our hearts. Suddenly we're able to see what has been lurking underneath the surface, because a lump of solid impure silver before heat is applied, just looks like pure silver externally, but when the heat begins to drive out the hidden dross from the innermost part of the silver, then it comes to the surface and we see it plainly.

Now, in the past, I have heard many times from the pulpit that the dross comes to the surface and you just skim it off, but this Jeweler friend of mine explained it very differently. She said that when you see the dross come to the surface in the crucible, then more intense fire is applied to the specific area where the dross is and finally it causes the bond between the silver ion and the dross to be broken and the silver ion, which is positively charged, let's go of the dross. The appearance of dross means the heat is turned up!

Because of the breaking of the bond, the negatively charged dross is driven away from the silver ion and it moves to the side of the crucible and fastens itself there. The thing about dross is that it needs something to attach itself to. If the silver is no longer holding onto or embracing it, it has to find something else to hold on to and the other most solid thing that it can find is the edge of the crucible and it stays clinging to the crucible. The silver particles, on the other hand, then become liquid and can move freely, energized by the heat energy imparted by the flames. You might feel like the fire is killing you, but it is actually empowering and separating you as you yield and submit to being purified.

Normally, when God begins to shine his spotlight on some issue, sin or character trait by bringing it to the surface, the stubbornness and self-will in us holds on to that dross. We don't want to let it go. We call it by any other name other than what it really is. We just do not want to admit the presence of the dross and it's almost as if we are embracing it and in an adulterous relationship with that dross, rather than in embracing Jesus, who is the Truth and the Light. So, the heat gets turned up and finally we can stand it no longer and just let go! When we yield and are not stiff-necked as our fathers were; when we come to the Lord in humble repentance and acknowledgment of our sin, we open our arms, let go of the dross and it is driven away from us as far as the east is from the west.

So, if you find the Lord bringing some negative thing to the surface in your life, realise that that's not the end of the process of purging that dross. Don't get disheartened when the fire gets hotter and hotter honing in on that particular thing, whether it's self righteousness or pride or unbelief or whatever. What God is doing is completely purging you of that dross. He's breaking the bond between you and that dark thing once and for all. If you desire to dwell with the everlasting burnings, take every thought captive to the obedience of Christ; humble yourself and repent as David repented and embrace the cleansing, refining process instead of resisting it, and that bond between you and that thing that has been a part of your life right up to this point, is broken. Thrust it from you, because when the silver begins to show the reflection of the Refiner on its surface, then He knows it's pure and its ready to be poured out of the crucible - and the dross is left behind in the crucible. It's not a part of you anymore. You're not going to struggle with that thing for the rest of your life if you will just co-operate with the applied intense heat in specific areas, until the root is dealt with. Then you are poured out, you are liquid, you are completely yielded and surrendered and you pass over the threshold and the cusp of the crucible into the next part of the process.

An interesting thing my jeweler friend also shared with me, is that when the silver is poured out of that crucible, the next place it goes to in its liquid form is a mould for whatever it is going to be made into, but what is interesting is that mould is also red-hot! This is because if you poured liquid, hot silver into a cold mould, it would spatter everywhere and be wasted, so the mould is heated as well, until there is no difference in the heat of the mould and the crucible. So the silver in its liquid state moves into a different situation, different circumstances - one that still feels very hot and yet nothing impure is coming to the surface any more. Once the silver is in the mould, it takes the shape of the mould as the temperature steadily drops. This cooling off and solidifying period is when we begin to realise the shape of what He is making us to be. And with this realisation comes understanding of purpose and function; knowledge of our place in the end-time army of God.

Opening and Shutting, Ruling in Your Metron

I really believe what God is doing with us through this of making us liquid (completely yielded to Him) is in order to pour us into a mould that makes an instrument, a key, and the key is the key to the House of David. The key to the House of David opens the front door of the House of David and the House of David is the corporate house from which

Christ comes forth or is made manifest in the earth. God intends Jesus to be made manifest in us.

Now a key is also a ruling weapon in a sense as it opens and shuts, cuts off and releases, separates and demarcates seasons and territories. With this comes reward and recompense according to the details of what has been endured in the previous chapter. Eliakim, the faithful servant in Isaiah 22:22, was raised up and given the key of David in order to rule the household and the daily activities that took place therein. His word carried authority. In the same way, the season of refining, of forging and shaping, of testing your mettle, has resulted in a metron of authority being attributed to your account. Your spoken word will carry authority in the spiritual realm that you have been assigned to rule in. This is why the heat of the fire has been cranked up so much in your life in the preparation season! God wanted you to carry more authority! He was using your uniquely orchestrated fiery circumstances with definite purpose in mind. He knew what the drawing board of Heaven has intended you to become in Christ.

The fire also breaks curses off your life. Where the enemy has surrounded you with thorns and biers to keep you from your future in the Kingdom, the raging fire of your God Who is a Consuming fire turns every obstacle in your path to ashes!

Hotter is Better

In July 2013, as I was pondering the intensity of the fiery trial I was undergoing, fully aware that there were many other saints who also had been put through an intense and difficult preparation process, I heard the Spirit say to me, "WHY ARE YOU IN THE FIRE HEATED SEVEN TIMES HOTTER?" I did not have an answer and He continued, "Because you refused to bow your knee to idolatry and evil, to go with the flow and follow the crowd, you refused to do what was safe and easy. God is demonstrating through your life what a vessel of honor looks like. He testing your mettle and you are the real deal - even unbelievers can see that now. Before this fiery furnace season you blended in with the crowd. Now you stand out like the stars on a moonless night. You carry the source of the light inside you. You don't reflect another's glory, you are a carrier of the glory of God and you will come out of this time with every bondage burnt off you and not one trace of the fire you have been through. There will be no permanent damage, not even the smell of smoke or singed eyelashes will be found on you. God has used your unswerving standard of righteousness and holiness as an opportunity to open unbeliever's eyes to see Christ in the furnace with you and it influenced the whole pagan nation. They couldn't see Christ before you went in the furnace. Sometimes, it is the furnace's effect on you that opens the eyes of the unbelieving."

That word empowered me to stand and endure the full preparation time. Did you know that sand is passed through fire 7 times hotter to make glass?! Full clarity and transparency is needed for glass to be useful in holding and displaying the contents within for the searching world to see.

The Fourth Man in the Fire

Remember the 3 men who were thrown in the fire heated seven times hotter in the Book of Daniel? It wasn't because they had sinned. On the contrary, they were devout and God-fearing men and would not be swayed by what was going on around them. They were not crowd-followers or people-pleasers. They lived for the smile of Heaven. Just like you, Beloved saint! So make peace once and for all with the fact that no wrong-doing of yours brought on this appointment with the raging fire. Instead, God allowed the enemy to be used as a tool to bring Him glory, to reveal your fellowship with Christ in the fire for all to see and to turn a whole nation to Him after the fire season.

Tested and Authenticated

Let's look a little more deeply into the trial of these men:

Dan 3:16 ,17,18 Shadrach, Meshach, and Abednego answered and said to the king, O Nebuchadnezzar, we have no need to return a word to you on this matter. If it is so that our God whom we serve is able to deliver us from the burning fiery furnace, then He will deliver us out of your hand, O king. But if not, let it be known to you, O king, that we will not serve your gods nor worship the golden image which you have set up.

These three men were not prepared to bow their knee to the gods of Babylon or the golden image which the king had set up. They were wholly faithful to God, no matter what the consequences were. They knew God was able to deliver them, but they did not demand that He do so. Their faithfulness to God was not dependent on Him coming through for them!

So often we are prepared to defend our faith IF God moves on our behalf. We will remain faithful IF He comes through for us. How many have turned their backs on God because He didn't perform according to their expectations, not realizing that their hearts were being tested in the process of the delay or absence of His visible workings. Beloved, we must determine to align ourselves with Truth because it IS Truth, no matter what the personal consequences are for us.

Dan 3:19 Then Nebuchadnezzar was filled with wrath, and the form of his face was changed against Shadrach, Meshach, and Abednego. He spoke and commanded that they should heat the furnace seven times more than it was usually heated.

Seven times hotter – a complete refining is commanded because of these young men's' unwillingness to bow the knee in idolatry. The king's face was changed towards them – in other words, his attitude toward them changed. Previously they had been set up in positions of authority in the business world of Babylon (v 12). Now suddenly they went from a position of favour and influence to being in disfavor.

In the church, there are those who have been put in positions of authority, ruling in the Babylonian religious system. However, they are true servants of God. There comes a day when they are faced with a choice – enter into idolatry and remain in favor **OR** remain faithful to the King of Heaven and lose position and influence in the religious system.

This choice is the preliminary test of those desiring to become vessels of gold in the Master's House. On making the right choice in God's eyes, they are not then rewarded (as is the way of man) but rather plunged into a refining fire seven times hotter than is considered a normal trial. Perhaps, Beloved, this will help you understand the journey you have travelled!

Dan 3:21 Then these men were tied up in their slippers, their tunics, and their mantles, and their other clothes, and were thrown into the middle of the burning fiery furnace.

These men were not tossed into the furnace naked. Every vestige of clothing they wore also entered the fiery flames. In the same way, everything connected to you – your spiritual giftings, mantles of authority and every area in which you function in the kingdom – is also destined to pass through a refining and testing process.

Remember that the clothing these young men wore was the clothing of Babylon. They had been functioning in delegated positions of power in the business sector of the Babylonian empire. Beloved, in order to be transformed into a vessel of gold, it has to be determined whether the garments you wear are truly God-appointed or bestowed by man. As Paul teaches, 'each one's work shall be revealed. 'For the Day shall declare it, because it shall be revealed by fire; and the fire shall try each one's work as to what kind it is' (1 Cor 3:13).

Dan 3:22 Then because the king's commandment was urgent, and the furnace exceedingly hot, the flame of the fire killed those men who took up Shadrach, Meshach, and Abednego.

The mighty men of Babylon were the ones to throw these three into the furnace. They represent principalities and powers who are appointed to harass and torment the servants of God, just as satan was given permission to attack Job.

However, the wonderful thing about the heat of the fiery furnace you have been thrown into, Beloved, is that it will destroy all those who have been arrayed against you. Every demonic messenger whom satan has assigned to bring about your destruction will be burnt up by the heat of the fire. And the ironic thing is that it was the king of Babylon who chose the measure of heat in the furnace! He had no clue his own mighty men would be consumed by the heat of that furnace. That which he intended for evil, God turned for good!

Dan 3:23 And these three men, Shadrach, Meshach, and Abednego, fell down bound into the midst of the burning fiery furnace.

These three faithful servants went into the fire bound. Not only were they bound but they fell down and were unable to help themselves. They must have experienced a moment of sheer terror and helplessness, being unable to do anything to shield themselves from the heat. However, Psalm 37:24 tells us that when a righteous man falls, 'he shall not be utterly cast down: for the LORD upholds him with his hand'. The flames dealt with the ropes binding them and they were lifted back onto their feet by an unseen hand.

Beloved, every form of bondage that the enemy has put on you before entering this fiery trial will be removed. He intended for the ropes to prevent you from helping yourself but the flames will deal with them. Every form of restriction that prevents you moving freely in your service of God will be dealt with during this time. You will emerge from this season with every fetter on your hands and feet completely destroyed. If the enemy had known what the fire would accomplish, he probably wouldn't have thrown you in or made it so hot! It is time to thank God for the results of this fiery furnace season.

1Pe 4:12 Beloved, think it not strange concerning the fiery trial which is to try you, as though some strange thing happened unto you: 1Pe 4:13 But rejoice, inasmuch as you are partakers of Christ's sufferings; that, when his glory is revealed, you may be glad also with exceeding joy.

We all know the old saying 'the proof is in the pudding'. It is all very well to have a wonderful sounding recipe but until it has been tried and tested, one is unable to confidently recommend it.

Well, Beloved, until we pass through the fiery trials we are no more than a recipe! Theoretically, we can state what we believe and who we are, but only the heat of the fiery trial will bring out the true character hidden within. For us to have the fragrance and flavour of Christ forged within our bones, we must pass through the oven. Our lives are to be living letters not just words on a page. Therefore we should not be shocked at the fiery furnace. God is intending to openly say over you, "This is MY beloved son, in whom I am well-pleased".

The Babylonian king issued the command to remove Daniel and His friends from the furnace. Those who have been in fire 7x hotter for a long season and now have the testimony that the 4th man is visible with them, will be released by the very king or demonic agent who sent them in. This is, in effect, the enemy's acknowledgement that nothing he threw at you could destroy your relationship and fellowship with Jesus and so he is calling the assignment to an end. You are released as a living testimony of the superiority and power of the God whom you serve and many around you will be impacted as a result.

Changing the Decrees of Darkness

Dan 3:28   Nebuchadnezzar spoke and said, Blessed be the God of Shadrach, Meshach, and Abednego, who has sent His Angel and has delivered His servants who trusted in Him, and has changed the king's words and have given their bodies that they might not serve nor worship any god except their own God.

Note that the king's words were changed. Beloved, there were decrees of death and destruction issued over your life by the enemy just before you entered the furnace. They were powerful and the elements were put in place for them to be carried out. However, God Almighty holds the power to change decrees issued in the spiritual realm. This is why no weapon formed against you can prosper – God uses the legal decrees issued against you and turns them for your good. The words of the king of darkness are changed in order to bring forth light in and through you!

Therefore there is never any need to fear the might of the enemy. Every judgment issued against you, you will show to be in the wrong (Isaiah 54:17 AMP). How? By the character you display in the furnace, by the life and virtue of Christ which is visibly seen in you even while you are in the midst of the fire. Therefore there is a day of vindication for you, a glorious afterward – a day when the enemy bows his knee and acknowledges that God loves you.

Recompense and Restoration

Dan 3:30   Then the king made Shadrach, Meshach, and Abednego prosper in the province of Babylon.

Following the fire there is a time of recompense, a time of restoration and prosperity manifested in your life – and God uses the enemy to bring it about! In just the same way as Mordecai was placed in a position of rule over the house of Haman and all his wealth, so too will the Lord bring you into a place of influence and cause you to prosper in the very realm where the enemy has ruled previously! You are going to be taking ground for the Kingdom of God and plundering the province of the enemy. He will have no option but to restore to you seven times what he stole in the previous season. In the same measure with which he heated the fire (seven times hotter) so will he be made to deliver recompense seven times more that you have lost. This covers every area of your life – emotional, relational, physical, financial, and spiritual.

Labels Consumed by the Flames

Dan 1:7 to whom the ruler of the eunuchs gave names. For he called Daniel, Belteshazzar; and Hananiah, Shadrach; and Mishael, Meshach; and Azariah, Abednego.

These men of God were given names in Babylon by the ruler of the eunuchs. In other words the enemy attached labels to them which were intended to render them incapable of bringing forth fruit. Eunuchs had the appearance of masculinity but had no ability to father children. However God knew their real names and the plans He had for them. Daniel means 'God has judged'. Hananiah means 'God has favored'. Mishael means 'who is what God is?'.Azariah means 'God has helped'. Their original names were a declaration of the work God would bring forth in their lives through the fiery furnace. They are a vivid depiction of judgment being given in favour of the saints!

Beloved, it doesn't matter what labels have been attached to you. It doesn't matter what words of death have been spoken over your potential to bear fruit. God will use the trial of the fiery furnace to break every limiting word over your life and bring forth your full potential in full sight of your enemies! They will be forced to acknowledge that their labels have not stuck! You are not who the enemy says you are.

Dan 3:27 And the satraps, the prefects, the governors, and the king's advisers gathered and saw these men on whose bodies the fire had no power (and the hair of their head was not scorched, nor were their slippers changed, nor had the smell of fire clung on them).

Beloved, in the day you emerge from the flames, every principality and power arrayed against you will gather and acknowledge that the fire has no power over you. More than that, the smell of the fire will not have clung to you. In other words, everything you have experienced in the refining process will remain in the closed previous chapter. Your hair, which represents the anointing on your life, will be in no way diminished or damaged. In fact, it will probably have grown during the trial!

There will be no vestige or residue of the trial upon you – so much so that people will find it hard to believe that you actually went through those terrible trials. You will be whole. There will be no sign of damage upon you. All those who saw you enter the fiery trial and know the details of your circumstances will stand amazed at what they see before their eyes - just as the disciples were dumbfounded when they saw Jesus in His resurrected whole body because they had seen the gory details of the crucifixion and the wounds inflicted upon him.

2. Plucking Firebrands from the Refiner's Fire

In Zechariah 3, Joshua the High Priest, who standing before throne in filthy garments, is described as a brand plucked from the fire. Joshua is a type of Jesus, so this mention of him in his high priestly office alludes to Jesus our High Priest who was after the order of Melchizedek. He represents a company of priests after this order who have been in the Refiner's fire and now stand before the throne having been plucked out of it. The state of the high-priestly garments gives satan opportunity to accuse this Melchizedek company but a rebuke comes from the throne.

This corporate priestly company is His choice. He has plucked them as brands from the fire. Throughout the refining fire season, accusation has resounded before the throne as more and more dross has come to the surface. And oh the accuser of the brethren has many minions working for him amongst the ranks of the so-called saints! But now there is a change of season. The accuser is silenced and the Father speaks words of affirmation; words of commendation, words which remove every last vestige of iniquity; words which close one season and release the beginning of another.

Zec 3:1 THEN [the guiding angel] showed me Joshua the high priest standing before the Angel of the Lord, and Satan standing at Joshua's right hand to be his adversary and to accuse him. Zec 3:2 And the Lord said to Satan, The Lord rebuke you, O Satan! Even the Lord, Who chooses Jerusalem, rebuke you! Is not this a brand plucked out of the fire? Zec 3:3 Now Joshua was clothed with filthy garments and was standing before the Angel [of the Lord]. Zec 3:4 And He spoke to those who stood before Him, saying, Take away the filthy garments from him. And He said to [Joshua], Behold, I have caused your iniquity to pass from you, and I will clothe you with rich apparel.

A firebrand is plucked from the fire with purpose in mind; firstly to prevent it being utterly consumed and destroyed by the flames, then to use it as a carrier of that same fire. It is used to give light and set others on fire according to the will of the one who wields it. This Melchizedek Company are to be firebrands in the hand of the Lord of Hosts.

Jesus came from the tribe of Judah; He was not a Levitical priest. Paul speaks of this change of priesthood in the book of Hebrews; the purpose was to bring forth a priesthood that functioned not according to the Law, but according to the power of an endless life. This is resurrection power; power that cannot be quenched or overcome by death. The Melchizedek priesthood will walk in this power in the end-times.

Zechariah mentions the tribe of Judah in chapter 12. God says He will regard the tribe of Judah with favour and 'open His eyes upon them'. Earlier, in chapter 3:9, Joshua is given a stone with seven eyes. This refers to an impartation of the seven spirits of God. Once again the removal of all iniquity in a single day is mentioned - a change of season from accusation to affirmation and endowment. The opening of God's eyes upon Judah refers to the outpouring of the seven spirits of God upon this newly robed company. Then He says something very interesting concerning the leaders of Judah:

Zec 12:6 In that day will I make the chiefs of Judah like a big, blazing pot among [sticks of] wood and like a flaming torch among sheaves [of grain], and they shall devour all the peoples round about, on the right hand and on the left; and they of Jerusalem shall yet again dwell and sit securely in their own place, in Jerusalem.

They will be like flaming torches among the sheaves, In other words they will set the sheaves of wheat on fire. They are also described as being like a pot of burning coals amongst the pieces of wood. Once again they are being used to ignite others.

In a sense, the Melchizedek kings and priests are being set aflame and used like the central candle of the menorah to light the rest of the branches of the candlestick. The shamash or servant candle is the one which is first ignited. It is a forerunner receiving the baptism of fire in order to set the others aflame. He makes His messengers flames of fire! Then they carry the message which imparts the fire to others. (You can read more about this in the last chapter of this book).

Fire in the Forests of Ministry

A few years ago, I visited a nearby Nature Reserve called Jonkershoek, meaning 'Young Men's Corner'. Normally, this area was filled with tall pine trees and indigenous fynbos vegetation native to the Western Cape province of South Africa, but this time it looked totally different. A fire had passed through the plantation a few months before and the scene was totally changed. Rain had since fallen and small clumps of grass and low fynbos bushes were sprouting but there was still marked evidence that the fire had visited this place. I could sense the Lord's presence and knew I was about to receive a lesson concerning the visitation of the spirit of judgment and burning to the church.

Isaiah 1 describes the refiner's fire passing through His church and the results this visitation brings forth:

Isa 1:25 And I will bring My hand again upon you and thoroughly purge away your dross [as with lye] and take away all your tin or alloy. Isa 1:26 And I will restore your judges as at the first, and your counselors as at the beginning; afterward you shall be called the City of Righteousness, the Faithful City. Isa 1:27 Zion shall be redeemed with justice, and her [returned] converts with righteousness (uprightness and right standing with God).

This is the Father's objective in sending the fire - to restore His Body to a state where they are again known as 'the City of Righteousness'. But in the process of bringing this about, there is also a purging and separation that inevitably takes place:

Isa 1:28 But the crushing and destruction of rebels and sinners shall be together, and they who forsake the Lord shall be consumed. Isa 1:29 For you will be ashamed [of the folly and degradation] of the oak or terebinth trees in which you found [idolatrous] pleasure, and you will blush with shame for the [idolatrous worship which you practice in the passion-inflaming] gardens which you have chosen. Isa 1:30 For you shall be like an oak or terebinth whose leaf withers, and like a garden that has no water. Isa 1:31 And the strong shall become like tow and become tinder, and his work like a spark, and they shall both burn together, with none to quench them.

At Jonkershoek, great trees were lying fallen and charred on the ground. Once, other saplings had sheltered in their shade, but now they lay like fallen giants, blackened and lifeless. And here the Lord began to speak to me about those with lofty ministries who have pridefully towered over others in the church. When the appointed visitation spoken of in Malachi 3 takes place, many of these will be hewn down and consumed by the flames.

One such tree that had fallen and been incinerated had left a blackened stump with the flame shape of a keyhole in it. The fall and judgment on large ministries which have been weighed in the balances and found wanting will also cause keys of revelation to be released and doors to be opened for those who up to this point have been faithfully serving God unseen and unnoticed or honored as members in the lowest ranks of these ministries. Just like God released His people from slavery in Egypt by a wave of judgments, so too the visitation of the spirit of judgment and burning will release those who have been slaves to the spiritual ambition and ministries of those who do not walk in the fear of the Lord. These will be released as flames of fire to fulfill the Kingdom works God has prepared beforehand for them to walk in.

When the Spirit was poured out on those in the upper room, flames of fire appeared on each of their heads and they tumbled out of that room into their Kingdom assignments, wreaking havoc on the religious strongholds of the organized ministry of the day. These

120 had been personally schooled by the resurrected Jesus for 40 days in the ways of the Kingdom and these teachings were diametrically opposed to the religious instruction being given by the Pharisees and priests.

Isaiah 6:13 tells us about a tithe that shall remain after a great tree has fallen, and this tenth will be eaten, bringing good spiritual nourishment. They are the holy seed:

KJV Isa 6:13 But yet in it shall be a tenth, and it shall return, and shall be eaten; as a teil tree, and as an oak, whose substance is in them, when they are felled or have cast their leaves: so the holy seed shall be the substance thereof.

During my visit to the fire-ravaged Jonkershoek, I also found one charred stump that had a star shape in its base and this space was filled with sand. The Holy Spirit reminded me about those who are the descendants of Abraham by faith, whose numbers shall be as the sands of the sea. Because of his obedience, God made a promise to Abraham that still holds true today: **Gen 22:17** that blessing I will bless you, and multiplying I will multiply your seed as the stars of the heavens, and as the sand which is on the shore of the sea. And your Seed shall possess the gate of His enemies. Gen 22:18 And in your Seed shall all the nations of the earth be blessed because you have obeyed My voice.

That star shape in the stump had been there all along but had never been seen or brought to light and into manifestation until fire felled the great tree. Some of Abraham's descendants by faith, which are represented by the sands of the sea are about to be released to shine like stars when they are unveiled from within the heart of mighty tree ministries that will not survive the fire. They will be known for their spiritual wisdom.

Dan 12:3 *And those who act wisely shall shine as the brightness of the firmament, and those turning many to righteousness as the stars forever and ever.*

When a fire passes through a field, it leaves behind charcoal and ash. But here in South Africa, in our indigenous fynbos vegetation, the heat of the flames also causes the seeds of our protea bushes to split open and germinate. Without fire, they lie on the soil sealed; their potential beauty arrested and waiting for the Refiner to pass by. We need the fire to pass through our lives as it ignites the germination of spiritual seed deep within.

Shaping the Flames of Fire

At Jonkershoek Nature Reserve, there were great rocks which had not escaped the raging fire. As I investigated, I discovered that shards of flame-shaped rock had been sheared off the big rocks by the heat of the flames. Their former resting places were still clearly visible on the surfaces of the giant rocks. Those saints who were part of the Rock which is Christ are not harmed by the Refiner's fire passing through the field which is His Church, but shaped and cut by the fiery flames. They are released as a chip off the old Block! This phrase is used to describe children who are just like their father. In other words, they are of the DNA of Christ; that same Rock from which living waters flowed to quench the thirst of the people of God in the wilderness.

Psalm 29 describes extensively the effects of the voice of the Lord. It has become one of my favourite psalms to use as a skeleton for praying over myself and others in the remnant. Verse 1 usually addresses the psalm to 'the sons of the mighty' but this is an incorrect translation because the Hebrew phrase for this is 'ben El' which means 'sons of Almighty God'... quite a difference!

The whole psalm has both the positive and negative effects of the sound waves of His voice as He thunders. Verse 5 describes the power of His voice breaking tall cedars, or big ministries. The ground of Lebanon (the heart is lebab in Hebrew) is shaken up and down in rolling waves as God's power deals with His people. Then we come to verse 7 which is the one I want to focus on here as we are discussing the flames of fire. The Jewish Publication Old Testament version puts it like this:

Psa 29:7 The voice of the LORD hews out flames of fire.

The Hebrew word for 'hew' is chatsab, and also means 'to quarry or engrave'. It describes the work of a stone mason. The flame-shaped shards that were hewed or quarried by the raging fire at the nature reserve depict the effect of the voice of the Lord as He comes to

powerfully deal with His set-apart ones. King James translates chatsab as 'divide' giving a sense of separation between son and son or sheep and sheep as Ezekiel 34:17-22 describes.

Verse 8 tells us He is shaking the wilderness of Kadesh with the sound waves of His voice. Kadesh means 'holy or set apart'. So this psalm is not speaking about the general, fleshly-minded, marginally committed believers. It is a description of the sifting and dealing which comes within His remnant as He appoints and engraves specific flames of fire. He is using the fire to shape every detail of these flames of fire.

He is engraving assignments upon the hearts of the fully surrendered ones who have made themselves ready but He is also cutting down some ministries that have planted themselves upon the heights in the remnant movement.

He is bringing some to birth and shutting down others. This is almost like taking a tithe of the tithe. Only the pure in heart will come through unscathed and chosen for endtime assignments. They will be sent forth as flames of fire, vessels carrying His voice or sound; the Word made flesh within them.

Jer 23:29 Is not My word like fire [that consumes all that cannot endure the test]? says the Lord, and like a hammer that breaks in pieces the rock [of most stubborn resistance]?

The Release of the Ezekiels

I received a word passed on from a friend as I was writing this chapter and it is so in line with what I am sharing that I feel pressed to share it with you. It is attributed to a woman called Jessica Sowards. Never heard of her? Well, that's great because she represents the nameless, faceless ones who are being released as endtime voices of power (She writes a blog called 'thehodgepodgedarling'):

'Right now, in the secret place, God is preparing a generation of Ezekiels. They are nameless, faceless voices. He is plucking them from office jobs and universities, from tattoo parlors and bars, from dry churches and kitchens where they cook dinner with a baby on their hip, from the mission field and the prayer room. He's whispering to them in the night, shaking their circumstances and erasing the lines of their neatly drawn comfort zones. They are learning to walk through fire. They are forsaking fear and falling madly back in love with their First love. They are being ruined to everything else, spoiled by His presence. They won't want the world ever again, not after what they've seen and felt Him do.

They will be a peculiar people, an upside down people. Turning the other cheek to their enemy, blessing those who curse them, giving everything they've got to those who can't give anything back. They will make Jesus' name famous by choosing the altar over the audience. They will live a laid down life, broken and poured out like an alabaster box. They will not forget what they were rescued from, and will live with reckless abandon for the one whom they call Savior.

They will raise an army of dry bones to life with the Power of the Almighty they've submitted to. Signs and wonders will follow them and favor will be bound to their heads. They are marked. They are bold. They will not shrink back. They are revival, burning hard and fierce. The fire in them is unquenchable. Just wait. When you hear their voices you will know that they are sent. You will know that they are chosen.

But right now they are silent, weeping between porch and altar, being firmly rooted in an eternal paradigm. They are being sandaled with readiness for the gospel of peace. And with those readied feet they will run over glass, coals, lava if they have to. They won't slow down. They won't draw attention to their own able feet but instead, they will proclaim that there is one on His way, one who they aren't worthy to tie the sandals of. Get ready, nations, this remnant is being prepared. They will shake the entire world. They will ask questions that demand answers, they will carry an anointing that cannot be denied. They will not relent in their cries for heaven and mercy and miracles. The Truth is in them, and it is stirring, building, nearing the moment that it breaks forth.

You'll know it's time when you hear their voices. The nameless, faceless ones…'

-Jessica Sowards

Flames of Fire that Hammer and break the Rock

When Antiochus Epiphanes desecrated the temple in 2BC and killed most of the priests, a group of mighty warriors decided to fight to get back their temple out of the hand of the pagans. They were called the Maccabees (which means 'hammer') and after some time they managed to finally win back the temple and cleanse and rededicate it to holy use. The feast of Hanukkah is connected to the miracle of the supply of oil that occurred during this victory. In the same way messengers who are flames of fire will cleanse and rededicate the temple of His Body to holy use. They will be like the faithful Zadok priests who taught the people the difference between the clean and the unclean; like Elijah who demonstrated to the people the difference between a true prophet of God and the prophets of Baal which had been feeding them up to this point. During these end-times, there will be a group of messengers of fire, consumed with zeal for His house, who wield the Word of God like a hammer which breaks the rock of resistance in pieces.

Flame of Fire Refuge

In 70AD, when the Romans destroyed Jerusalem, a group of warriors and some faithful saints fled the Romans and hid in a mountain-top fortress called Masada. Here they held out for 3 years against the Roman attempts to build a ramp to reach and destroy them. What is amazing is that when viewed from the air, Masada is in the shape of a flame! What a prophetic picture of those faithful to the One True God during the end-time revival of the Roman Empire. The saints that lived on this hilltop fortress preferred to die rather than surrender to the Romans and similarly, many sincere Believers will be martyred for their faith rather than deny their Beloved Savior during the tribulation period. It is recorded that only two women and 5 children survived as all the others had laid down their lives voluntarily at Masada, rather than be killed by the Roman army who was building a ramp to the top of the fortress. When the Romans finally broke through their defenses, they found that all but this handful had taken one another's lives rather than die by a Roman sword. These two women and five children are a type and shadow both of the two witnesses who will go forth from the place of death and preach a message of repentance during the 3&1/2 years of tribulation, and also of the five loaves and two fishes who were used by the Lord to feed the multitude in a wilderness place.

3. The Man of Fire

Towards the end of May in 2016, I surfaced from sleep in the morning watch and heard, 'MY SERVANT WILL BE A BURNING OVEN PURIFYING THE SILVER VESSELS' and as I heard this, I saw an image of a man with flames from the waist down.

I was also given understanding that the phrase 'My Servant' was referring to the Branch, mentioned in Zech 3:8. I fell asleep again and on waking, I could again smell smoke and burning in the passageway of my home. I was reminded of my experience many years before of the arrival of the Spirit of Judgment and Burning for an appointed season or passage of time where purging and purifying would take place.

The man with fire from the waist down is mentioned in the Book of Ezekiel as he had a vision of the glory of God at the river of Chebar during the Babylonian captivity. (The fire of God is connected to the glory of God). On the throne that he saw in the midst of the glory was a Man:

Eze 1:27 From what had the appearance of His waist upward, I saw a lustre as it were glowing metal with the appearance of fire enclosed round about within it; and from the appearance of His waist downward, I saw as it were the appearance of fire, and there was brightness [of a halo] round about Him.

So it is this Man Who is coming to be an oven purifying the silver vessels. Below the waist of the body are the loins; the area where the seed of the Man is formed and sent forth. The fact that there is fire from the waist down speaks both of the purifying and purging of the seed and also the release of the seed as flames of fire.

The seed are the sons of God, carrying His spiritual DNA, and all the earth groans while waiting for their manifestation or appearance. The fire of purging and purifying occurs for a passage of time and then comes the release of fiery messengers; sons fit to take over their Father's business. The Book of Daniel describes a scene depicting this release. He too was shown the throne of God;

Dan 7:9 I kept looking until thrones were placed [for the assessors with the Judge], and the Ancient of Days [God, the eternal Father] took His seat, Whose garment was white as snow and the hair of His head like pure wool. His throne was like the fiery flame; its wheels were burning fire. Dan 7:10 A stream of fire came forth from before Him; a thousand thousands ministered to Him and ten thousand times ten thousand rose up and stood before Him; the Judge was seated [the court was in session] and the books were opened.

A stream of fire is issuing forth from the One on the throne; a river of fiery messengers going forth burning with zeal for His house. But first comes the time in the oven and the purifying of the silver vessels.

As mentioned in chapter 1, during this time, all that does not align with His expressly written will for each seed (each son or daughter destined to become a flame of fire), is purged and removed.

During worship, I heard a song being sung by a number of voices. I assume they were angelic voices singing over the remnant:

River of the burning Son,

let Your fiery breath now come,

come and set Your living stones on fire,

Jealousy as strong as death,

come now with Your fiery breath,

come and set Your living stones on fire,

seven eyes and seven horns,

Lamb with fiery love that burns,

come and set Your living stones on fire'

The Corporate Man of Fire

The forerunner company has undergone this time in the oven already, in preparation for release as a corporate 'man of fire'; a company of servants who make up His servant, the Branch. This company is then used to kindle a fire in the earth and their release comes after their own personal long night of trial. In order to be able to be a part of this corporate 'Man of Fire', one has to be able to endure the fire, pass through it and not be burned. This requires a certain level of purity and godliness. In Isaiah, a question is asked:

Isa 33:14 The sinners in Zion are afraid; trembling seizes the godless ones. [They cry] Who among us can dwell with that devouring fire? Who among us can dwell with those everlasting burnings?

Please note it is the sinners IN ZION who are concerned they may not be able to survive the fire! Yes, it is disturbing that there are sinners found in Zion but this is exactly why the Refiner's fire comes - both to purge the dross within individuals and to purge the imposters from Zion. The Lord answers the question concerning who is able to dwell with the everlasting burnings:.

Isa 33:15 He who walks righteously and speaks uprightly, who despises gain from fraud and from oppression, who shakes his hand free from the taking of bribes, who stops his ears from hearing of bloodshed and shuts his eyes to avoid looking upon evil. Isa 33:16 [Such a man] will dwell on the heights; his place of defense will be the fortresses of rocks; his bread will be given him; water for him will be sure.

Purity of heart, mouth and deed provides immunity from the flames of the everlasting burnings. God's throne is a fiery flame and if we intend to be seated in heavenly places in Christ at His right hand, we had better be able to dwell with the everlasting burnings!! In fact, when one is made a flame of fire, you have become of the same substance as the God Who is a consuming fire!

Malachi 4 speaks of the coming of a Day that burns like an oven in which the wicked are severely dealt with. During this time, those who fear His Name are released and tread the wicked down as ashes. Ashes are only present when fire has passed through an area and it is obvious that those who are released have not been consumed by the fire. They are the very flames which tread the wicked down and reduce them to ashes.

Mal 4:1 FOR BEHOLD, the day comes that shall burn like an oven, and all the proud and arrogant, yes, and all that do wickedly and are lawless, shall be stubble; the day that comes shall burn them up, says the Lord of hosts, so that it will leave them neither root nor branch. Mal 4:2 But unto you who revere and worshipfully fear My name shall the Sun of Righteousness arise with healing in His wings and His beams, and you shall go forth and gambol like calves [released] from the stall and leap for joy. Mal 4:3 And you shall tread down the lawless and wicked, for they shall be ashes under the soles of your feet in the day that I shall do this, says the Lord of hosts.

This company, the Branch, will be used to rebuke and call people to repentance for 3&1/2 years; their fiery words bringing separation between the wicked and those whose hearts respond to the call to return to the Lord.

Isa 66:15 For behold, the Lord will come in fire, and His chariots will be like the stormy wind, to render His anger with fierceness, and His rebuke with flames of fire.

It is significant that Ezekiel saw the vision of the fiery throne when the Israelites were captive in Babylon, as it speaks of the Man of fire coming as a carrier of the portable throne of God to visit the people of God who have allowed Babylon or the world and its ways to enter the Church and now find themselves utterly captive. The details of this visit are detailed in Malachi chapter 3. Later on, in chapter 8 of Ezekiel, this same Man of Fire lifts the prophet by the hair and reveals to him the reason for the fiery judgment that is coming upon His people.

He shows Ezekiel a graphic depiction of what is going on within the hidden chambers of the elders and leaders of His people. In other words, He is coming to deal with the idolatry and defilement taking place within their own minds. *These* are the secret chambers that other men cannot look into, but God has been a silent (and disgusted) viewer for many years!

Eze 8:2 Then I beheld, and lo, a likeness of a Man with the appearance of fire; from His waist downward He was like fire, and from His waist upward He had the appearance of brightness like gleaming bronze. Eze 8:3 And He put forth the form of a hand and took me by a lock of my head; and the Spirit lifted me up between the earth and the heavens and brought me in the visions of God to Jerusalem, to the entrance of the door of the inner [court] which faces toward the north, where was the seat of the idol (image) of jealousy, which provokes to jealousy.

Eze 8:9 And He said to me, Go in and see the wicked abominations that they do here. Eze 8:10 So I went in and saw there pictures of every form of creeping things and loathsome beasts and all the idols of the house of Israel, painted round about on the wall. Eze 8:11 And there stood before these [pictures] seventy men of the elders of the house of Israel, and in the midst of them stood Jaazaniah the son of Shaphan [the scribe], with every man his censer in his hand, and a thick cloud of incense was going up [in prayer to these their gods]. Eze 8:12 Then said He to me, Son of man, have you seen what the elders of the house of Israel do in the dark, every man in the chambers of his imagery? For they say, The Lord does not see us; the Lord has forsaken the land.

He goes on to show Ezekiel that His people are worshipping the gods of Babylon as well as the Sun and so He has no alternative but to begin judgment with His house. Straight after this vision, God gives the command to mark those who weep over the abominations that His people are committing in order to protect them and then He releases His angels to slay the idolaters, beginning at His sanctuary.

The Fiery Girdle of Truth

There is something significant about the waist of the Man of fire. This is the demarcation point of the area of the everlasting burnings. Above the waist, he appears bronze like molten, glowing metal which has emerged from the fire, but from the waist down, the fire doesn't go out. If you do a study of the word 'everlasting' in the Bible, you will find it connected to covenant, glory, light, joy, dominion, heavenly dwellings, truth and faithfulness. All these things are the portion of those who walk in the fear of God and live to do His will. They are those who have been weighed in the balances and found fit to be released as His fiery seed into the earth. Isaiah 11:2&3 describes both Jesus, the Pattern Son, and the sons of God who will be manifested in this last hour. And, interestingly, His waist is mentioned in this description:

Isa 11:5 And righteousness shall be the girdle of His waist and faithfulness the girdle of His loins.

The cut-off points for the choice of those who are able to dwell with the everlasting burnings are righteousness and faithfulness. Melchizedek means 'King of righteousness' or 'righteous king'. So these ones who dwell with the everlasting burnings are part of the Melchizedek priesthood, released to rule and reign in the earth.

The waist or loins are involved in the swearing of oaths, the making of covenants and the release of fruitful seed. When the saints of old were about to die, they called their children and made them swear oaths concerning the disposal of their remains and thereafter released a prophetic blessing upon each child, before passing away. In essence, they were passing the baton of blessing from one generation to another of righteous seed.

Before His death by crucifixion, Jesus did an interesting thing. He removed His outer garment or mantle, signifying the anointing or ministry He had walked in up to that point and instead girded Himself with a bondservant's towel.

Joh_13:4 ...Got up from supper, took off His garments, and taking a [servant's] towel, He fastened it around His waist.

He was moving from the place of rabbi or teacher to the place of a bondslave. In today's terms, we would say He was changing hats, but back then, one's girdle signified position and authority and this removal of one garment and the donning of the servant's towel as a girdle signified something shocking. Jesus, the Head and Living God, assumed the role and function of the lowest servant. The Head of the Body became lower than the feet in order to wash the Body with the cleansing water of His words. Just like the saints of old, He was passing on the baton from one generation to another and the servant towel girdle indicated the change of era and the changing of the guard. He was showing them how to participate in His everlasting covenant. The washing of the feet allowed them to have a part in Him, or in other words, to participate in sharing His inheritance.

Joh 13:1 [NOW] BEFORE the Passover Feast began, Jesus knew (was fully aware) that the time had come for Him to leave this world and return to the Father. And as He had loved those who were His own in the world, He loved them to the last and to the highest degree. Joh 13:2 So [it was] during supper, Satan having already put the thought of betraying Jesus in the heart of Judas Iscariot, Simon's son, Joh 13:3 [That] Jesus, knowing (fully aware) that the Father had put everything into His hands, and that He had come from God and was [now] returning to God, Joh 13:4 Got up from supper, took off His garments, and taking a [servant's] towel, He fastened it around His waist.

A Changing of the Guard

We are presently in the season of the changing of the girdle of the Body of Christ from the teacher/rabbi girdle to the bondslave girdle. In other words, those who are recognized as learned and anointed teachers in the Body, who have instructed the Body in the last season of preparation are being laid aside or laid to rest, and the bondslaves who have no rank or fame in the present Church system are being strongly girded around the Body in this hour, in order to release the teaching and word for this appointed moment in the Kingdom. They have understanding of the times and know what the Body needs to do in order to be found positioned rightly in Him in order to have a part in His inheritance. They are sent forth from the Man of Fire, a fiery girdle of messenger bondslaves. They know who they are, where they have come from and where they are going and their meat is to do the will of Him who sent them and to complete it.

The Hebrew word for girdle is an interesting one. It actually means 'manacles or chains' which connects us to the bondslave theme, and it comes from a root word meaning 'a flash of fire or a burning arrow, a firebrand'. So here we have the confirmation that the messengers who are flames of fire form this girdle with which Jesus equips Himself just before the days of His suffering and death.

The waters they wash the feet of the Body of Christ with are fiery waters; waters which separate and challenge; waters which convict, intended to cleanse the dust of the journey from the feet. Dust speaks of flesh as the first man's flesh was made from the dust of the earth. Dust speaks of the ways of fleshly men. The waters of the Word released will cleanse the outer court of the temple of God, just as Jesus drove out all fleshly activities from the outer court of the temple; the outer court representing the Body. As Malachi 3 says, this time, Jesus is coming in His end-time messengers as a Refiner's fire and a fuller's soap. And these messengers know what they are talking about. In fact, their lives are the message. The Word has become flesh in them. They don't speak in lofty words of men's wisdom but in a demonstration of the Spirit and power and the Lord works with them, confirming the Word with signs and wonders.

A Prophetic Day of Atonement

When the High Priest performed the duties of the Day of Atonement, He first sprinkled the Holy Place and its furniture with the blood of the sacrificed bull in order to cleanse it. Then he took a bowl of fresh blood from the slain goat for the sin offering and sprinkled it on the mercy seat. The Blood of Him who is the Aleph, the Head must cleanse the Holy place of His temple. Then the mercy seat can be cleansed.

Lev 16:33 He shall make atonement for the Holy Sanctuary, for the Tent of Meeting, and for the altar [of burnt offering in the court], and shall make atonement for the priests and for all the people of the assembly.

The Holy place speaks of those in the Body who are living for the Lord, set apart and holy to the Lord. They are doing their best to be faithful and walk according to Spirit. Yet, we all fall short and are in need of cleansing, just as the disciples had walked daily with Jesus but needed their feet washed in order to have a part in Him or share the fullness of inheritance in Him. Jesus, our High Priest enacted this principle when He cleansed the temple before offering His own Body and Blood as a sacrifice for the sin of mankind. In this day, the Holy Place, His set apart ones must be cleansed before crossing through the veil to dwelling in the Most Holy Place, where the glory of God is the only light.

A Jewish Bride has a mikvah or cleansing bath on the day of her wedding. This usually occurred after a private feast with the Bridegroom after midnight, so in the morning watch as the Sun was rising, she bathed. This was in effect to present her to her husband without spot or wrinkle. The Day of Atonement is called Yom Kippur by the Jews and another name for it is 'Face to Face'. It depicts the shedding of blood which seals the covenant of marriage when a newly married husband and his virginal wife are face to face in sexual intimacy. It is a day of total oneness, one flesh and when applied to our spiritual relationship with the Bridegroom, alludes to becoming completely one in Spirit. But prior to this must come a last cleansing, a mikvah for the Bride.

Washing by Sons, not Servants

Interestingly, during the ancient Jewish wedding ceremony, the groom would remove the bride's sandals, wash her feet and then place a new pair of sandals upon her feet. Sandals speak of inheritance. This new pair of sandals purchased by the bridegroom says that all he has is hers; that she now shares in his inheritance and wealth from his father. When Jesus was washing the disciples' feet, first their sandals had to be removed. Then their feet had to be washed, not by a servant but by the Son. In the same way, in the season of washing of the feet of the Body that is now at hand, the removal of the sandals of a past season and the pouring of cleansing water will be done by the sons of God, not the servants in the house. These are the waters of completion; the final releasing of the waters of Truth needed to complete the work the Spirit began in the preparing of the Bride for her Bridegroom.

Waters Which Shake the Holy Ones

In psalm 29, the effects of the voice of God are described and one of the things that are mentioned is that His voice shakes a certain wilderness:

Psa 29:7 The voice of the LORD engraves the flames of fire. Psa 29:8 The voice of the LORD shakes the wilderness; the LORD shakes the wilderness of Kadesh.

The sound of His voice carried in the waters that wash the feet in this hour will shake the wilderness of Kadesh. Kadesh means 'holy, set-apart, consecrated'. Does this describe the place where you dwell? His cleansing waters are coming to wash you and they will bring a shaking. It is the shaking that assembles the dry bones in the valley which Ezekiel looked upon. It is the shaking which assembles bone upon its bone and lays sinews upon them. It is the shaking which puts together the great end-time army of God in preparation for the great infilling of the seven Spirits that equip this mighty warrior company to stand upon its feet and go forth under the command of their God.

Remember how John the Baptist described himself as a voice crying in the wilderness, "Prepare ye the way of the Lord"? (Mark 1:3) Once again, there is going to be a sound released in the wilderness of Kadesh, in the Holy place and it is going to be a sound of preparation. We know from Acts that the group of people who served God during the days after Jesus' ascension were called 'The Way':

Act 9:2 Saul asked from him letters to Damascus, to the synagogues, so that if he found any being of the Way, both men and women, having bound them he might bring them to Jerusalem.

The voice that shakes the wilderness in these days will be sent to prepare those of The Way; those who walk in the good old paths. And those who are carriers of this sound will walk in the anointing of the Spirit of Elijah. They will not have all the trappings that have gone with the big ministries of the past season. They are the nameless, faceless ones who move at the sound of His voice; the flames of fire sent to prepare the Way for the coming of the Bridegroom. They are friends of the Bridegroom and are trustworthy to complete the last washings of preparation.

There is a very interesting passage in Ecclesiastes 12 which is traditionally believed to be speaking of get old. However, when I looked at it recently, the Holy Spirit showed me something else hidden in the folds of the words used.

Ecc 12:1 Remember then your Creator in the days of your youth, before the evil days come, and the years draw nigh, when you shall say: 'I have no pleasure in them'; Ecc 12:2 While the sun, or the light, or the moon, or the stars, be not darkened, nor the clouds return after the rain: Ecc 12:3 In the day when the keepers of the house shall tremble, and the strong men shall bow themselves, and the grinders cease because they are few, and those that look out of the windows be darkened

Joel 2 speaks of the day of the Lord as being a day when the sun and moon are darkened and the stars do not give their light. So this passage above is referring to the time just before that, at the brink of its start. There is a warning to remember the Lord; to bring Him to mind before the days of evil and before the clouds return after the rain. By now we are familiar with the concept of the clouds being a type of the cloud of witnesses who bring the heavy latter rain. These clouds are going to return to their place once the latter rain is released. And what does this deluge of water do? It makes those in charge of the house shake! This water of the Word is shaking everything that can be shaken so that only what cannot be shaken, remains.

And more than that, it has an effect on the strong men or, more accurately, strongmen of that house. The word for 'bow themselves' in Hebrew also means 'to be overturned'. So we see that the waters carry a sound which makes the leaders of a certain house shake and it overturns the strongmen assigned to that house. So what house is it talking about? Well, the key is found in the word 'grinders'. This Hebrew word is very interesting because it means 'to grind meal' but the root word means 'to behave as a concubine'!! This is not the house of the true Bride. This is the counterfeit house that does not give the saint Bridal rights but keeps them as a concubine grinding out meal for the leaders of the House of Babylon, meeting their needs and being at their beck and call, with no legal rights or standing in the house. They are there to be used at the leaders' pleasure.

Praise God, the waters released as a deluge by the bondslave sons washes the filth of this counterfeit house off the feet of the Bridal Company and institutes their true bridal inheritance sandal rights. Off with the concubine sandals and on with the inheritance sandals. The house of concubines is being shaken by the sound of these waters and the strongmen that have held the saints captive as concubines are knocked flying; their assignments cancelled! Remember how Jesus made a whip and overturned the moneychanger's tables and drove the sellers of doves out of the temple? The voice of the Lord is shaking the Wilderness of Kadesh and dealing with all who call themselves members of the Bridal Company, and a separation and clarification is going to be evident. No more pretenders in the Holy Place of His temple.

The other thing that happens after the heavy latter rain is poured out is dealing with those who look out of the windows (Eccle 12:3 ... *those that look out of the windows be darkened)* It was Jezebel who painted her eyes and looked haughtily out of the window as Jehu rode in, carrying a double portion anointing. It was the last time she would look down on anyone. She was thrown to her death by the very men she had reduced to eunuchs. They were galvanised to life and power by the sound of Jehu's words. And all it took was one action of cooperation with the direction of that sound and they were liberated from slavery to witchcraft's whims. All those who have eaten at Jezebel's table and helped in the making of eunuchs of those intended to be fruitful sons of God will have all spiritual light removed from them as judgment falls. Their lights will be put out. Their lamp-stands removed from its place. Such will be the power and anointing of the sound which the girdle sons of God carry.

The Private Love Feast with the Lamb

Remember the disciples' feet were washed during the private love feast with the Lamb in the upper room which had been furnished and prepared for that purpose. Interestingly, that actual room in Jerusalem is quite dark and not much can be made out upon the walls but recent sightings with ultraviolet light revealed a lamb sculpted in the centre of the domed ceiling. As the bridal company is ministered to and washed in the prepared upper room, the Lamb who has been slain, the One with seven eyes and seven horns, is presiding over the proceedings and you will be washed with sevenfold light in the day when he binds up the wound of His people and heals the scars you have accumulated on the journey to this place.

Here you will feast upon the Lamb who is your Passover and partake of the Blood of the Bridal covenant. You are the firstfruits company, those who are given understanding and sevenfold light and truth; your portion of the inheritance you share with your Bridegroom before the transaction is completed openly for others to see and experience. At a Jewish wedding in ancient times, the Bride and Bridegroom would complete their vows and do the foot-washing, take of the cup of wine of the covenant together and then retire to a private chamber to become one. Then they would return after 7 days to enjoy the wedding feast with the guests.

The Tender Washing of the Wife

Ephesians 5 speaks of Christ's love for His Church as the love of a husband for a wife. He washes her with the water of the Word and presents her to Himself, cleansed and without spot. And in this end-time, the water of the Word is on fire! Paul tells us that fire will test all we have built in our lives and Jesus Himself spoke of the visitation of fire upon every Believer:

1Co 3:13 the work of each will be revealed; for the Day will make it known, because it is revealed in fire; and the fire will prove the work of each, what sort it is.

Mar 9:49 For everyone will be salted with fire, and every sacrifice will be salted with salt.

Fire will not only burn up wood, hay and straw but will reveal His jewels. At present, the building with wood and straw in the Body of Christ is obscuring the gold and the silver vessels, but, oh, when the fire comes, all that is not of Him is removed out of the way. All that releases a mixed and impure sound is silenced and then His jewels can be openly displayed.

Mal 3:17 And they shall be Mine, says the Lord of hosts, in that day when I publicly recognize and openly declare them to be My jewels (My special possession, My peculiar treasure). And I will spare them, as a man spares his own son who serves him. Mal 3:18 Then shall you look back and discern between the righteous and the wicked, between him who serves God and him who does not serve Him. Mal 4:1 For behold, the day comes that shall burn like an oven, and all the proud and arrogant, yes, and all that do wickedly and are lawless, shall be stubble; the day that comes shall burn them up, says the Lord of hosts, so that it will leave them neither root nor branch.

Oh how we need the day that burns like an oven. How we need the waters of the fiery bondslave girdle company. How we need the separation and clarification and unveiling that only the flames of fire messengers can ignite! How we need the shaking of the Holy Place, the sprinkling of the sound of cleansing Blood carried in the waters of the Word released by the Sons who have been set in place around the waist of the Body of Christ. These are those in whom the Father is well-pleased; the ones ready to take over their Father's business - and their task is the final touches of cleansing preparation to make the Bride ready.

The Righteous Flaming Arrow

One night a few years ago, I surfaced from sleep only to hear a command, "Release a righteous arrow over the congregation". I had no idea what the Lord meant until I discovered that the Hebrew word for girdle also means 'a flaming arrow'! The time of release of His messengers who have become flames of fire can also be described as releasing a corporate righteous arrow over the present-day church. The sons of God are the righteous arrow girdle that is released by the voice of the Father to minister to His congregation. Arrows are also mentioned in the wedding psalm, psalm 45 and, once again, righteousness is a prevailing theme in the release:

Psa 45:4 And in Your majesty ride on triumphantly for the cause of truth, humility, and righteousness (uprightness and right standing with God); and let Your right hand guide You to tremendous things. Psa 45:5 Your arrows are sharp; the peoples fall under You; Your darts pierce the hearts of the King's enemies. Psa 45:6 Your throne, O God, is forever and ever; the scepter of righteousness is the scepter of Your kingdom.

The flaming ones are His corporate arrow released and sent forth as lightening flashes in battle. They shall be defended and protected as they go forth driving the influence of the enemy out of the midst of God's people. This girdle or arrow belt of Truth shall wash the feet of the Body so that they may participate in the fullness of their inheritance in Christ. Victory is sure because the Lord fights with the arrow company. The sound of the righteous arrow must be released over the congregation as the Lord decreed in order to release the waters of cleansing.

*Zec 9:14 And the Lord shall be seen over them and **His arrow** shall go forth as the lightning, and the Lord God will blow the trumpet and will go forth in the windstorms of the south. Zec 9:15 The Lord of hosts shall defend and protect them; and they shall devour and they shall tread on [their fallen enemies] as on slingstones [that have missed their aim], and they shall drink [of victory] and be noisy and turbulent as from wine and become full like bowls [used to catch the sacrificial blood], like the corners of the [sacrificial] altar. Zec 9:16 And the Lord their God will save them on that day as the flock of His people, for they shall be as the [precious] jewels of a crown, lifted high over and shining glitteringly upon His land*

When a child is born or brought into manifestation, the feet are the last part to emerge from the womb of preparation. There have been many generations of holy believers who have walked this earth and are now with the Lord and part of the cloud of witnesses. We are the final portion of the Body of Christ, destined to live in these end-times and witnessing the fulfillment of all that has been written. In essence, we are the feet of the Body; the last part of the Bridal body of Christ (flesh of His flesh) and those who have gone before do not come to perfection apart from us.

The Burning Arrows on Assignment

In the first chapter of Ezekiel, he is with the captives in Babylon (notice sometimes God allows the prophet to also be taken captive in order to have a true mouthpiece amongst His captive people). It is significant that he was 30 years old at this time as this is the age when a son is eligible to take over his father's business. Ezekiel had obviously been found ready as this vision is the beginning of the delivery of a message to the people in captivity to Babylon. This faithful man is given a vision of the arrival of the glory of the Lord in a whirlwind of fire. Out of the midst of this glory came living creatures, which I believe is a depiction of the corporate assembly of the manifest sons of God. They come forth from the glory as carriers of the glory and they are led only by the Spirit of God:

Eze 1:12 And they went every one straight forward; wherever the spirit would go, they went, and they turned not when they went. Eze 1:13 In the midst of the living creatures there was what looked like burning coals of fire, like torches moving to and fro among the living creatures; the fire was bright and out of the fire went forth lightning. Eze 1:14 And the living creatures darted back and forth like a flash of lightning.

Can you see these sons of God releasing flashes of heavenly revelation, depicted by the lightening? And there is fire everywhere. These are the messengers who are flames of fire!

Eze 1:24 And when they went, I heard the sound of their wings like the noise of great waters, like the voice of the Almighty, the sound of tumult like the noise of a host. When they stood, they let down their wings. Eze 1:25 And there was a voice above the firmament that was over their heads; when they stood, they let down their wings.

This fierce fiery company carries the sound of many waters, the voice or sound of the Almighty. Over them there is a voice giving them instruction and assignments, which they carry out immediately for they are bondslave sons. And the waters they pour out are waters of cleansing and a call to repentance for filthy ways walked in. May the feet of the Body submit to their cleansing.

4. Consummation ~ a Bridal Fire Offering

I have always loved the types and shadows hidden in the Word of God. And how precious it is to have a veil lifted and to see another one hiding in plain sight all the time! During the instructions for consecration and ordination of the priesthood in Exodus 29, there is a veiled picture of the wave offering of the Bride and her complete union with the Bridegroom. In the last months, I have written extensively on the barley firstfruits company (these writings can be found on my Fresh Oil Releases Wordpress site). Now in this type, God speaks of wheat. This, however, does not preclude those relating to the barley firstfruits company. Jesus Himself used different types and pictures to represent Himself; all referring to different aspects of His character. On occasion, He was 'the Door or 'the Good Shepherd'. At other times He referred to Himself as 'the Bread of Life'. In the same way, this picture and type concerning 'wheat bread' can also apply to the same company as those termed 'barley firstfruits'. In this type and shadow, the baptism of fire is depicted.

First one ram is prepared and offered as a burnt offering. We know the ram is a picture of Jesus because the ram was provided as an alternative to sacrificing Isaac. The Bridegroom Ram is waiting for us in the midst of the flames of fire, consumed with love for His Bride. Then instruction is given concerning the grain part of the wave offerings:

Exo 29:2 And unleavened bread and unleavened cakes mixed with oil and unleavened wafers spread with oil; of fine flour shall you make them. Exo 29:3 You shall put them in one basket and bring them in [it], and bring also the bull and the two rams;

No leaven is contained in this wave offering; all are made from FINE flour and 2 of the 3 portions have oil – one has oil in the dough and the other, a wafer, is anointed on top. The oil symbolizes the involvement of the Holy Spirit in this ordination. The bread with oil inside represents the baptism in the Holy Spirit, which is the earnest or down-payment of our inheritance. The wafer is baked without oil, but the oil is applied just before the ordination process. It is the oil of consecration.

All these offerings are to be made with wheat, a connection to Pentecost or Shavuot and the wheat harvest when the offerings of grain are to be in the prepared state – it is not enough to grow to maturity; grinding, sifting, absorption of the water of the Word and time in the fire are all imperative before consecration and ordination to appointed position can occur. Remember also that Pentecost is the time when flames of fire appeared on the heads of each disciple as the Spirit was poured out. Shavuot was the betrothal ceremony at Mount Sinai when the Lord came down in a cloud with fire.

Let me digress a little… last night I had the strangest dream. I was looking in on a very festive gathering in a darkened room, where a large sheep and goat were in the middle of the partying crowd. They had been dressed in royal robes and the people were putting crowns on their heads. I was shocked in the dream that the people could see no difference between a sheep and a goat and were indiscriminately bestowing both with ruling powers. The church has become so worldly that there is a lack of discernment as to who are really sheep or goats; who are wheat and who are tares. However, the One Who sits on the throne has no such problem. I believe that this reference to wheat in the ordination of the priests is a reference to true believers, no messengers of satan masquerading as angels of light. Remember also that Baphomet is depicted as having the head of a goat and Jesus is represented by the Ram, or leader of the flock of the Father's sheep. The thought that this is occurring in the church is very disturbing…Anyway, back to the ordination in Exodus 29…

The omission of leaven in this bread of ordination is a reference to purity and a lack of sin or hypocrisy (the leaven of the Pharisees). Remember also that all leaven is removed from the houses before Passover and there are seven days of unleavened bread which follow the Passover. So the Lord seems to be bringing Passover and Pentecost together in this priestly ordination. Pentecost or Shavuot is in the 50th day after Passover, speaking of Jubilee or full freedom from slavery to the world and Babylon. The ordination is for those that are fully separated unto the Lord,

I see in the description of the basket of bread, a shadow of all the virgins in the book of Esther, who have gone through the preparation and purifying processes to become a candidate for the choice of queen. They are placed together in one basket before the Lord and then one of each kind is chosen and taken out and waved or lifted up together before the Lord.

Exo 29:23 And one loaf of bread, and one cake of oiled bread, and one wafer out of the basket of the unleavened bread that is before the LORD:

The whole basket of bread is not waved, just 3 selected portions. In other words, out of the whole basket of prepared, unleavened bread, only a small number, a 3-in-1 company are selected to be waved and then go on to be an offering made by fire. Many are called but few are chosen. Even after the time in the fire, the grinding and sieving and more time in the furnace, there are still some who are not selected. However, those who are chosen go on to represent all those who are unleavened bread before the Lord. They become the offering made by fire and dwell in the everlasting burnings but this firstfruits portion represents the whole prepared waiting basket.

Exo 29:24 And thou shall put all in the hands of Aaron, and in the hands of his sons; and shall wave them for a wave offering before the LORD. Exo 29:25 And thou shall receive them of their hands, and burn them upon the altar for a burnt offering, for a sweet savour before the LORD: it is an offering made by fire unto the LORD.

Leviticus describes the consecration of the priests in more detail:

Lev 8:26 And out of the basket of unleavened bread, that was before the LORD, he took one unleavened cake, and a cake of oiled bread, and one wafer, and put them on the fat, and upon the right shoulder: Lev 8:27 And he put all upon Aaron's hands, and upon his sons' hands, and waved them for a wave offering before the LORD. Lev 8:28 Then Moses took these things from their hands and burned them on the altar with the burnt offering as **an ordination offering**, *for a sweet and satisfying fragrance, an offering made by fire to the Lord.*

We see it is actually Moses (representing the Law or the Heavenly Court) who selects one of each of the 3 types of bread offerings. There is a legal transaction going on here, during and after selection. Examination as to quality precedes selection. Those chosen and favored are part of the Bridal company (remember Esther found favour with the king more than all the other women and he placed the royal crown upon her head). Then Moses places the 3-in-1 company on top of all the fat from the ram, which represents connecting them to the fullness of anointing of the Ram, in other words, the seven spirits of God, which Jesus, the Ram of God walked in.

Moses then placed the fat and the bread on the right thigh (or shoulder, as the Hebrew indicates). The shoulder of the Ram indicates His authority, so those selected from the basket of unleavened portions are connected to the same delegated power and authority as the Bridegroom, to operate in the seven spirits of God. Note also that it is the right shoulder, associated with the strong right arm of the Lord and the sons of the right hand, who are deemed fit to take over their Father's business. The bread, fat and shoulder are then handed to the Aaronic priests to wave before the Lord.

Then they are again taken by Moses out of the hands of the Aaronic priesthood and lowered into the flames. In other words, this bridal wave company complete with authority and anointing are acknowledged and lifted above those present, surrendered to the Lord and then 'taken out of their hands' or 'separated from the religious system and the influence of the priests' and put into the fiery flames to become one with the Bridegroom.

It is not the Aaronic priests who give this woman to this Man to be wed. It is Moses, the one who led God's people out of a system of slavery; the one who talked with God face to face and brought the sapphire tablets with the engraved marriage covenant down from Mount Sinai; the one who led the people of God to the edge of the Promised Land before stepping aside – like the father of the bride who leads his daughter to her face to face appointment with the waiting groom at the altar.

Bride of Christ, do not look to men in ministry to bring about this union and consummation of marriage covenant with your Bridegroom. Do not look to a priesthood after the order of Aaron to complete the spiritual transaction you long for. You need a higher authority to hand you over to your Groom; you are a priestly Bride after the order of Melchizedek and are destined to become perfect in one with your High Priest after the order of Melchizedek. Let your Father, the Ancient of Days who sits upon the throne, present you to your Bridegroom.

A Woman on Fire

The Hebrew word for 'offering made by fire' (ishshah Strongs 801) means 'sacrifice or burnt offering' and is written exactly the same as the word used for 'woman' in Genesis 2 when God made a woman for Adam. So this offering made by fire also depicts the woman God has shaped for His Son. Ishshah comes from the word Esh-shah (Strongs H800), which is a feminine form of the word for 'fire'. God is definitely emphasizing the feminine aspect of this ordination offering. So this offering made by fire, this Bridal wave offering is a corporate company of messengers who are flames of fire. Not only this, but they have become fully one with their Bridegroom; the One Who has eyes of fire and they can now dwell with the everlasting burnings.

'...*Then Moses took these things from their hands and burned them on the altar with the burnt offering as* **an ordination offering**, *for a sweet and satisfying fragrance, an offering made by fire to the Lord.*

The word translated 'ordination offering' in Hebrew also means 'a setting of gems'. Beloved, this baptism of fire, this consummation is also the process of your being set in place as one of His jewels.

A Threefold Feast of Love

'...*one loaf of bread, and one cake of oiled bread, and one wafer*...This 3-fold offering is 3 different representations of harvested grain that has been prepared for this occasion of consecration and ordination. The word translated 'loaf' in Hebrew also means 'to dance or whirl, round, a tract of land especially the Jordan Valley, a talent'. So the first round loaf mentioned connects us to the Jordan valley, to the completion of the circle of the wilderness journey and the subsequent crossing of the Jordan into the land of Promise.

The second oiled 'cake' (which is also round and pierced) connects us to the anointing contained within the vessel, which is intended for the outpouring to the benefit of others. The piercing represents the fellowshipping in His sufferings in order to be made into His likeness.

Then the wafer with oil spread on top is indicative of consecration and anointing into office or appointed position. So this 3-in-1 wave offering represents the Bride who is crossing the Jordan, having completed the full circle of the wilderness preparation and is now entering the Promised land of her inheritance, endued with the seven spirits of God and functioning in her delegated Kingdom authority. She is prepared to be seated at the right hand, ruling and reigning from the fiery throne. She has made herself ready and after being presented as a wave offering, is transformed into an offering made by fire;

coals of fire consumed with zeal for His house and ready to be released as messengers of fire into the earth.

Fused in the Fire

The Bride does not fear being immersed in the fiery flames on the altar because she has already been through the process of the refiner's fire during her preparation season. This fire is different. This is Holy Fire and the adding of the wave offering to the burning ram causes the two to become one; a fusing together with bonds that cannot be broken, and this union releases a sweet and satisfying fragrance to the Father. Bear in mind that 'to be consumed' or to partake in 'consummation' means 'to be utterly given to, to perfect, to complete', even as a bride and her groom become one physically and the union is consummated. Involved in this fusion of two into one is a release of seed, the DNA of the Bridegroom containing the blueprints and instruction which produce great fruitfulness.

May the Lord add understanding to this beautiful picture in His Word.

Radiating Revelation Light

The Lord often has me acquire objects at His leading and only afterwards explains why they are in my possession. On one such occasion fairly recently, He prompted me to buy 3 crystals. Now please don't think I am headed into the new age jungle. God Himself created crystals; we just don't subscribe to all the new age witchcraft which others use them for.

Two of these crystals were flame-shaped aura crystals, in colors of deep blue, gold, green, red and bronze. The word 'aura' is used today in spiritualist circles, but actually comes from the Latin meaning 'breeze, wind, the upper air' and in Greek, it means 'air or breath that comes from above'. It is not the smog-ridden air of the human plane.

The Hebrew word 'or' means to set on fire, to kindle, to shine' and there is another Hebrew word 'orah' which sounds exactly like 'aura' which means 'sparkling light'. My two aura crystals symbolise messengers who are flames of fire, carrying breath from the upper atmosphere of Heaven; the breath of God Himself.

Glorious Garments

I discovered that aura crystals are created by taking clear quartz and placing them in a closed environment with an electrostatic charge, which deposits layers of titanium and gold ions onto the surface of the crystal without damaging it. This does not affect the quality of the quartz underneath but the crystal shines with amazing rainbow colours. Titanium has an atomic number of 22. So what the Spirit showed me is that when we are shut in with the Lord for a season, worshipping in His presence with the power of the Holy Spirit all around us, we are busy receiving our new garments. They are applied layer upon layer by the words of His mouth. The Hebrew alphabet has 22 letters from which all the words written in the Word were constructed and as the sound of these letters is released from God's mouth (carried by His breath), they form a garment of glory clothing us. The more time we spend shut away in His presence, the more layers are laid down. This is why Moses' face shone when he came down after 40 days of speaking uninterrupted with God.

The third crystal I bought was silicon carbide. It is black and sharp and is a mineral which is remarkably common in space; a common form of stardust around carbon-rich stars. It is used in the making of bullet-proof vests and electronic devices which need to operate at very high temperatures or voltages. What does this tell you? This crystal has incredible endurance and strength and is very adaptable. It is comfortable in the height of the heavens and the depth of the fire and its environment does not change its characteristics. What a good description of those who have been through the fire heated seven times hotter and not even their hair has the smell of smoke.

In a sense, the 3 crystals depict the 3-in-one unleavened bread offering after they have been through the application of fire. They come forth bearing the glory; vessels wearing new garments and possessing incredible strength. They operate in the spirit of might as they execute His will on earth as it is in Heaven.

5. Messengers who are Flames of Fire

What is a flame of fire made of? The process of combustion produces heat and light energy which is seen as the colors of the flame, which is in the gaseous (or spirit) state. In other words, flames are a form of energy or power which can move freely without being contained by boundaries or parameters. When God makes His messengers flames of fire, He is releasing power through them in the form of light and revelation as they are led by the Spirit of God. Coupled with this is the heat of passionate love for His house or temple; the Body built for His Son. When God turns up the heat in people's lives, accompanied by increased light to see their situations clearly, it brings them to the place of making a choice - to love truth and return to full alignment with God's standard and plumbline or to harden their hearts and turn away. Those who do the latter are walking away into the dense darkness that is creeping over the earth and will end up taking the mark of the beast as their minds have become darkened.

Deut 4:24 and Hebrews 12:29 tell us that our God is a consuming fire, referring to His jealous love and zeal to bring about His purposes in the earth. When He makes His messengers flames of fire, they too are filled with this fire of passionate zeal for His purposes and His house. Zeal is fiery jealous love in action; jealous because that which is rightly His has been injured or removed from Him in some way. When Jesus made a plaited whip and cleansed the temple, his disciples knew it was the zeal or fiery love for God's house that was motivating Him:

Joh 2:14 There He found in the temple [enclosure] those who were selling oxen and sheep and doves, and the money changers sitting there [also at their stands]. Joh 2:15 And having made a lash (a whip) of cords, He drove them all out of the temple [enclosure]--both the sheep and the oxen--spilling and scattering the brokers' money and upsetting and tossing around their trays (their stands). Joh 2:16 Then to those who sold the doves He said, Take these things away (out of here)! Make not My Father's house a house of merchandise (a marketplace, a sales shop)! Joh 2:17

And His disciples remembered that it is written [in the Holy Scriptures], Zeal (the fervor of love) for Your house will eat Me up. [I will be consumed with jealousy for the honor of Your house.]

When I wrote the book of End-time Wine, the Spirit showed me that the cleansing of the Temple by Jesus described in the gospels was connected to the visit of the Lord to His people in Malachi 3, where it is mentioned He comes as a Refiner's fire and a fuller's soap. I was also shown that this end-time cleansing of the outer court of the temple would be accomplished by the plaited 3-fold whip or cord put together by Jesus. These 3 parts comprising the cord would be His fire, His light and the end-time wine imparted to a company of messengers who would also be consumed with zeal for His house. Jesus will be seen in this company or cloud of witnesses.

According to Mark 11, Jesus cursed the fig tree, plaited this whip and drove out all who were connected to merchandising the temple 3&1/2 days before He uttered the words, "It is finished" and yielded up His spirit on the cross. What occurred in these 3&1/2 days before His death give us some measure of the pattern which will unfold in the 3&1/2 years of the ministry of the two witnesses. Then they too will be killed and lie dead for 3&1/2 days like Jesus, before being raised to their feet alive and then ascending to the Father before the eyes of those watching, fulfilling the pattern lived out by Jesus.

These Two witnesses are the sons of oil spoken of in Zechariah, the two menorahs which receive a constant supply of oil from the two branches of the olives trees. Of course, the menorahs full of fresh oil must be lit or anointed with flames of fire like the 120 in the upper room in order to be able to impart the light-bearing potential of the oil they carry within. There must be a point of combustion for these end-time messengers to become flames of fire. Jesus spoke of this fire being ignited on the earth:

Luk 12:49 I have come to cast fire upon the earth, and how I wish that it were already kindled!

Why did He wish it were already kindled or ignited? Because the time of its kindling would signify the release of the two sons of oil, those two companies of end-time messengers filled with zeal for His house. They will go forth in the spirit and power of Elijah. Being added together, their two portions of anointing signifying the release of the double portion mantle (Elisha) upon those who have been privately trained as understudies in their wilderness season by the same spirit of Elijah. For 3&1/2 years, the call to repentance will go forth through these messengers. The whole earth will be bathed in the sound waves of one last call to return to the God from which all men came, through the Door of His Son.

The Hebrew word for fire is 'esh', written אש aleph shin. Aleph is the first or chief letter of the alphabet, representing the leader or head. Shin is also used to represent the name of God, so we see that the word for fire itself represents our leader, the only true God, who is a consuming fire.

The Hebrew word for man or husband is 'iysh', pronounced 'eesh'. Your heavenly husband, your Eesh, will make you into a flame of fire, an esh. Iysh is written aleph vav shin, so the only thing needed to change a man to a flame of fire is the removal of the vav. Vav denotes the connection of earth and heaven. Once you become a flame of fire, a messenger of fire, you are no longer earthly. You dwell fully in heavenly places.

This is important because of what we are told in Rev 12. When the woman flees to a place where she is fed and kept safe for 3&1/2 years, the dragon and his angels are cast to earth where he rampages against those who have the testimony of Jesus. But those who dwell in the heavens are safe as he has been removed from their place of residing. His accusations against them have been silenced:

Rev 12:12   Therefore be glad (exult), O heavens and you that dwell in them! But woe to you, O earth and sea, for the devil has come down to you in fierce anger (fury), because he knows that he has [only] a short time [left]!

Dwelling in heaven does not mean your feet have left the earth. It does not mean you have been raptured and escaped everything that happens in the end-times. It means you walk as Jesus walked; seated in heavenly places and fulfilling the Father's will upon the earth, operating in the seven spirits of God, which is the fullness of your inheritance. It means you are living out psalm 91, dwelling in the secret place of the Most High with angels protecting you in all your ways of obedience and service. It means no end-time plague or wave of destruction shall come near your tent (your body) as you witness the reward of the wicked. To dwell in Hebrew means 'to settle down and marry' and so psalm 91 is essentially a description of those who have become fully one with the Bridegroom, the One who has eyes like a flame of fire. They can dwell with the everlasting burnings because they have passed through and been purified in the Refiner's fire.

Fire in the Beginning and the End

And the LORD God formed the man from the dust of the ground, and breathed into his nostrils the breath of life; and the man became a living soul.
(Genesis 2:7)

As I said previously, the Hebrew word for fire is אש (esh). Derived from this two letter parent root is the three letter child root איש (iysh) meaning "man". The first man was created in the image of God, Who is a consuming fire. Before He fell, Adam was a fiery light being. That garment of light was lost or extinguished when they sinned. All that remained was the miniscule spark of light that lights every man. Of John the Baptist, it was written:

Joh 1:8 He was not that Light, but was sent to bear witness of that Light. Joh 1:9 That was the true Light, which lights every man that comes into the world.

Every living man still has an ember deep within waiting to be rekindled by an encounter with the Spirit of the God who is both fire and light.

The fullness of rekindling is the baptism of fire, where we operate not only in the Spirit of the Sovereign Lord but also in the other six spirits of God - the fully lit menorah. This is in essence the full return to the garden of Eden, the Second Adam bearing the image of the heavenly (1 Cor 15:49).

A man named Jeff Brenner gave me marvelous insights into the "creation" of fire from the ancient Hebrew's view or perspective, and also linked it to the creation of man.: 'In ancient times before the invention of lighters and matches, fire was made with a "bow drill" and tinder. The tinder is any fine organic material such as dried grass or inner bark fibers. The bow drill consisted of four parts, the fireboard, bow and string, rod and handle. The fireboard was made of a flat board with a v-shaped cut at the edge of the board. The bow and string is constructed similar to an archers bow. The rod is a round stick pointed at one end and rounded at the other. The handle is a flat round board. Fine tinder is compressed into a ball and layed on the ground. The fireboard is placed on top of the tinder with the v-shape cut over the tinder. The string of the bow is wrapped once around the rod and the pointed end of the rod is set on the fireboard over the v-shaped cut. The handle is placed on top of the rod. One hand holds the handle while the other hand moves the bow back and forth in a sawing motion. This action causes the rod to spin back and forth on the fireboard, causing friction in the rod. As the rod spins on the fireboard, fine wood dust is shaved off the rod and deposited in the v-shape cut on top of the tinder. The friction of the two woods rubbing also created heat causing the dust to become very hot. After a short time working the fire drill smoke will begin to rise from the heated dust. The fireboard is carefully removed leaving the pile of smoldering dust on the tinder. The tinder is picked up and enclosed around the dust and the fire maker blows on the dust increasing the heat. The dust then ignites the tinder creating fire. Let us now look at a passage in Genesis 2:7 in light of the ancient form of making fire, with God being the Fire-maker:

Genesis 2:7

Creator	Fire-maker
And the LORD God	And the fire maker
formed the man from the dust of the ground	formed a man of dust on the tinder
and breathed into his nostrils the breath of life	and he blew into the tinder the breath of life
and the man became a living soul.	and the man became a living fire.

Kindling the Fiery Ones

There is a moment when fire is ignited, when a flame of the match or candle touches the substance waiting to be ignited. Zooming in very close, one would witness an encounter where the state of one is imparted to the other. When Adam was ignited, it was the breath of God which filled him. Before this, he was perfectly formed with every part for function in place but all was still and lifeless. It took the life-filled breath of the Ruach or Spirit of the God who is a consuming fire to raise him up, fully empowered. The impartation of the breath of God is the impartation of power.

Humanly speaking, when a person has had a heart attack and died or drowned, someone must administer mouth to mouth resuscitation in order to impart breath or life into the body. A kiss is also administered mouth to mouth. No wonder the Bride in Song of Songs asks the Bridegroom to kiss her with the kisses of His mouth. There is an impartation of life and power with His kiss. All that is dead within, is raised up by the kiss of Life.

Psalm 2 describes the day of the kings of the earth assembling against God just after He has installed His Son on His holy hill. It is also a veiled description of the manifestation of the sons of God in verse 7 as He affirms them on a particular day and in verse 8, offers the nations as their inheritance. Then the last verse says this:

Psa 2:12 Kiss the Son, lest He be angry, and you perish from the way, when His wrath is kindled but a little. Oh the blessings of all those who flee to Him for refuge!

'Kiss the Son'... the word for 'kiss' in Hebrew means 'to touch, to equip with weapons, to rule'. It is written identically to another Hebrew word meaning 'to set on fire, to kindle'. When we kiss the Son, we are equipped with weapons, empowered to rule and set on fire! There is an impartation of fiery light from the mouth of God.

Sought Out and Sent

I would like to share a vision I received during worship in November 2018. I saw the heavens open; it appeared as if double doors got folded back and a beam of golden light shone down through that open door. I saw it going all over the earth like the powerful beam of a searchlight and I heard the following scripture spoken:

2Ch 16:9 For the eyes of the Lord run to and fro throughout the whole earth to show Himself strong in behalf of those whose hearts are fully His.

And I knew Heaven was looking for these ones who had completed their preparation and had undivided focus, looking only at the Bridegroom. In the above scripture, the words 'show himself strong' can be translated as 'to take firm hold of' and 'blameless' in Hebrew also means 'perfect, complete, wholly toward'. So the eyes of the Lord are going forth to take firm hold of those whose hearts are completely ready and focused toward Him and His purposes.

Then my attention was drawn to one whom had been discovered to be in such a condition and the beam of light narrowed and concentrated into a laser beam and ignited that one's heart into a small flame (I could see that there were others scattered here and there undergoing the same process, but apart from this, the earth seemed cloaked in twilight). Then I saw the wind begin to blow around that person and increase in strength, until it became a whirlwind around the person and this fanned the flame into a raging fire. I somehow knew that person was being made a messenger of fire and I heard the phrase 'turned into fragrance by fire'. I knew from previous study that this phrase was the meaning of the Hebrew word 'qatar' (H6999), which also means 'to smoke, to kindle or to offer incense'. What I saw taking place was the baptism of fire upon a person whose life was surrendered as a living sacrifice and prayer at the golden altar of incense.

In like manner, this depicts the fire from Heaven consuming the sacrifice of Elijah; an OT type of the Spirit of Elijah who has been preparing the Bride in the evening watch, as darkness begins to fall on the earth. The fire fell to confirm that Elijah was God's servant and had done all according to His word and express instruction. Likewise, the fire kindled upon the one whose heart had been found to be fully His indicates that this person is the servant of the Lord and has been obedient to everything which Heaven has instructed them to do. Elijah had his prepared sacrifice drenched with 12 jars of water. So this one who is ignited with fire from heaven has a heart saturated with the water of the Word. They are a living sacrifice, part of the company of people mentioned in Psalm 110 who offer themselves willingly in the day of His power. They surrender wholeheartedly; they are those whose hearts are perfect toward Him, who are completely His. And as the fire from Heaven consumed Elijah's sacrifice, they are consumed by the fire from His eyes of fire and the fragrance of this offering rises toward Heaven as a beautiful fragrance, acceptable to God.

After this, I was shown the origin and top of the search beam in the Heavens. There I saw ribbons of light in the seven colors of the rainbow being poured into that solid wide light ray; they were mingling and joining to form that golden beam and I knew that the seven colors of light I had witnessed were the seven Spirits of God which are described in Isaiah 11. I understood that the baptism of fire which I witnessed involved the outpouring of these same seven Spirits upon those whose hearts were fully His.

I was suddenly reminded of a mini vision I had at the beginning of the worship session. I had seen an outpouring out of Heaven onto the earth of various coloured flames of fiery burning coals. They did not look transparent and ethereal as flames usually do but seemed to contain great substance. At the time I had thought of the scripture in Revelation 8, where much incense is added to the prayers by the angel and then a censer of fiery coals is cast upon the earth. So I quickly looked up the scripture:

Rev 8:3 And another angel came and stood at the altar, having a golden censer; and there was given unto him much incense, that he should offer it with the prayers of all saints upon the golden altar which was before the throne.

I asked in my heart where the angel had got the 'much incense' because it seemed to be a separate substance to the prayers of all the people of God – and immediately I was brought back to the scripture in Songs 5:1 – ' *I am come into My garden, My sister, My Bride. I have gathered My myrrh with My spice…*' I knew in a flash of understanding that the large amount of incense had been gathered from His 'spouse', from the hearts of those who were fully prepared; those who had been found by the seven eyes of the Lord to be completely His. It is from this Bridal Company that the fragrant incense is sourced and mingled with the prayers of all the saints waiting for answers. This bowl of prayers is upon the golden altar, but the answers cannot be released until the 'much incense is gathered and this cannot occur until those who offer themselves willingly are completely ready.

Rev 8:4 And the smoke of the incense (the perfume) arose in the presence of God, with the prayers of the people of God (the saints), from the hand of the angel. Rev 8:5 So the angel took the censer and filled it with fire from the altar and cast it upon the earth. Then there followed peals of thunder and loud rumblings and blasts and voices, and flashes of lightning and an earthquake.

It is only as the smoke of this incense rises as a pleasing fragrance before God that the angel is released to cast the censer of fire upon the earth. And the results are earthshaking! What follows is a release of sound or 'voices' and lightning flashes and thunder. As the Bride's preparation is complete and the fiery baptism occurs, it ushers in a release of 'voices'; like John who was a voice crying in the wilderness to prepare the way of the Lord, so too these 'voices' or messengers are sent forth all over the earth to bring in the final harvest. These messengers of fire bring lightning or flashes of revelation that light up people's understanding, where minds have previously been darkened. The entrance of His Word brings light.

Thunder always follows lightning. Thunder is light converted to sound. The Greek word for 'thunder' also means 'roar'. So the revelation light released by these messengers of fire ushers in the roar of the Lion of Judah and a mighty earthquake is triggered. Prison walls shake and chains fall off and those trapped in darkness are brought forth to freedom. There is a mighty sound and light bombardment upon the bastions of the enemy and prison walls come tumbling down. Ancient rusty gates spring open. Once again, a corporate voice will be heard in unison all over the earth, "The Spirit of the Lord is upon me, because the Lord has anointed me … to proclaim liberty to the captives and the opening of the prison…"

The turning into fragrance by fire of the incense gathered from the Bridal hearts brings release to the whole Body, whose prayers have been waiting for answers. Those of you who have been in fires heated seven times hotter have endured it for the purpose of the Word you carry within your hearts. The true words of the Lord are pure words, like silver refined in the furnace of the earth, purified seven times. This speaks of seven cycles of cleansing and refining; seven testings to achieve and certify authenticity and purity. You are the real deal!

Many imposters and charlatans have deceived and used and abused God's people and brought the church into disrepute in the earth but now the vessels hallmarked by Heaven, sealed with His seal, are now to be released. The fire seven times hotter has been for the purpose of removing the dross from our hearts, so that only the pure silver of the Word remains – and it is this pure Word that provides the silver river for the forming of the chalice. Nothing you have been through has been without purpose. Nothing you have suffered is of no avail. Heaven has needed pure silver vessels for this endtime work. And you are of those who offer themselves willingly in the day of His power. From the womb of the morning will spring forth His holy vessels, scattered like dew all over the earth. Hear His roar, "Behold My beloved sons and daughters, in whom I am well pleased! Hear them!"

Fiery Sons or Fullers Soap

I discussed the river of fire in the chapter on The Man of Fire but I want to look at those verses in Daniel again and point out something else

Dan 7:10 A stream of fire came forth from before Him; a thousand thousands ministered to Him

and ten thousand times ten thousand rose up and stood before Him; the Judge was seated [the court was in session] and the books were opened.

Do you notice that only a small portion were ministering to Him, as his servants, and the rest were standing were standing before the throne for judgment? In fact, those ministering to the Ancient of Days upon the throne are one tenth of the number standing before Him. This speaks of a tithe having been taken; a company of people who have been examined and tested and found faithful. Like the Zadok priests who were appointed the privilege of coming near to Him and dealing with the choice things because they had remained faithful while others had gone into idolatry, this tithe company. In Ezekiel 40:46, we are told the Zadok priests have chambers with a view to the north and they are appointed to have charge of the altar to minister to the Lord and deal with the holy things. They are allowed in the Holy Place where the light of the seven spirits of God from the golden lampstand illuminate. They are allowed to eat of the showbread, properly in Hebrew 'the bread of the Presence'.

Eze 44:16 They shall enter into My sanctuary; and they shall come near to My table to minister to Me, and they shall keep My charge.

However, the rebellious, all those who have gone into idolatry, allowing other things to take the place of God in their hearts are weighed and found wanting and banned from the Holy place.

Eze 44:12   Because [the priests] ministered to [the people] before their idols and became a stumbling block of iniquity and guilt to the house of Israel, therefore I have lifted up My hand and have sworn against them, says the Lord God, that they shall bear the punishment for their iniquity and guilt. Eze 44:13 And they shall not come near to Me to do the office of a priest to Me, nor come near to any of My holy things that are most sacred; but they shall bear their shame and their punishment for the abominations which they have committed. Eze 44:14 Yet I will appoint them as caretakers to have charge of the temple, for all the service of the temple and for all that will be done in it.

The Spirit of Judgment and Burning brings separation between priest and priest and only those who are appointed to come NEAR to Him in intimacy are made into flames of fire, to form the river of fire, the fiery sons of God that flow from the throne. They are protected during the 3&1/2 years of tribulation spoken of in Rev 11. The other priests are relegated to the outer court of the temple which is appointed a trampling:

Rev 11:1 A REED [as a measuring rod] was then given to me, [shaped] like a staff, and I was told: Rise up and measure the sanctuary of God and the altar [of incense], and [number] those who worship there. Rev 11:2 But leave out of your measuring the court outside the sanctuary of God; omit that, for it is given over to the Gentiles (the nations), and they will trample the holy city underfoot for 42 months (three and one-half years).

Tread Out the Dirt in Those Garments

When the garments of the priests were washed, they were trampled underfoot, using fuller's soap to remove the dirt. Malachi 3 tells us the Lord is coming to His temple as both a Refiner's fire and Fuller's soap, to cleanse the sons of Levi that they may offer offerings in righteousness. The period of trampling of the outer court is a time of opportunity for those who have gone astray to come to repentance and return to the Lord.

In the Spirit's message to the church of Sardis, the cleanliness of their garments is spoken of. This is speaking to the cleanliness of life and the holiness of our walk with God.

Rev 3:4 Yet you still have a few [persons'] names in Sardis who have not soiled their clothes, and they shall walk with Me in white, because they are worthy and deserving. Rev 3:5 Thus shall he who conquers (is victorious) be clad in white garments, and I will not erase or blot out his name from the Book of Life; I will acknowledge him [as Mine] and I will confess his name openly before My Father and before His angels.

The majority of those in the church in Sardis had soiled their garments by their fleshly lifestyles. They are told in verse 2 to wake up and repent because nothing they have done has been acceptable to God, even though they carry the name of being alive. Judgement begins with the house of God and the outer court of His temple; Believers who walk after the flesh and not after the Spirit will have their garments trampled in the hope of returning them to whole-hearted allegiance to the Lord.

6. Set on Fire as the Darkness Falls

Isaiah 60:1 & 2 speaks of a time when the glory of the Lord is arising on a people even as dense darkness is falling on the earth. For those who have remained faithful and have already passed through the Refiner's fire, a time of carrying His glory is appointed. Yet, we do this in the midst of a darkness that is so thick, it can be felt. We carry the fire and glory light of God in our earthen vessels and consequently are a light in the darkness which draws others to Him.

A little while ago, I was worshipping at the piano and received a vision, accompanied by a very encouraging message. I saw many hundreds of angels, flying fast, having been dispatched with scrolls to the Bride and then each one standing like a town crier in front of one of the Lord's beloved, as they read in a sing-song voice to each one:

Hear ye, hear ye, one and all,

Hear the true words of the Lord,

hear ye, hear ye , precious Bride,

Take my counsel deep inside.

It grows dark increasingly

And you're battling now to see,

But remember light I've sent,

Words I whispered just for you,

Fan that flame alive again

Come now light the hearth within.

Fan My words into a fire

Stoke the flames of your desire
For My presence and My might,
Be now filled again with light.
Hold onto My promises,
Be not swayed by what you see,
For all the words I spoke are true
And the Daystar shines in you.
Fan My words into a fire,
Rise and shine this darkening hour,
Carriers of Truth for Me
Be now filled with much glory.

Hear ye, hear ye, precious ones,
The soon coming of the Son
Hear the angels shout the news
See the Daystar rise in you,
There is darkness all around
Men's hearts fail, but hear the sound
Of what Heaven is doing this hour
See My hand now move in power.
Hear ye My word from the throne
I am watching o'er My own.
I will keep you from the trial

That's appointed those not Mine
And I'll bring into plain view
Those who worship Me and do
Everything I've asked them to,

Those who love and fear Me
Shall now bear My full glory.
Carriers of Heavenly light,
Beacons in the darkest night,
Showing others how to be
Righteous once again in Me.
Stars who shine are now to be
Full revealed for all to see
Holy vessels brought to sight
Full of power and of might,
Working Kingdom strategies
Watch and see the darkness flee.
It's now coming time to shine,
Fan your flame and show you're Mine.
Do not shake as others do
Focus not on daily news,
But on who I Am in you
And see what your God will do!

Unveiled to Shine at the Appointed Time

Something very interesting occurred in Israel the week before Hanukkah 2017 and the Lord began to show me prophetic parallels in it for those who are appointed to be set on fire. A seven year old girl, Hadas, and her mother Ayelet Goldberg – Keidar went for a walk in the historic Beit Shean Valley. They were climbing the mounds near Kibbutz Nir David when Hadas noticed a pottery vessel lying near the mouth of a cave. It turned out to be a rare, intact 2,200 year old clay lamp. They took it to an archaeologist who confirmed it was from the historical period known as the Maccabean Wars against the Greeks. The Maccabees were a group of warriors who fought to regain the temple after it had been completely defiled (by slaughtering a pig on the altar) and its menorah extinguished by the Greek leader, Antiochus Epiphanes.

The archaeologist also told Hadas and her mother that a porcupine digging out its den for the winter was responsible for the excavation of the lamp and added that porcupines prefer archaeological sites because the earth is less packed due to man's activities in the past.

It is no coincidence that the Lord brought this particular clay lamp to light at this specific time in this place, near a kibbutz which means 'lamp of David'. The Word tells us:

Pro 20:27   A person's spirit is the lamp of the LORD; it searches throughout one's innermost being.

We carry the treasure of the knowledge of the glory of God in our earthen or clay vessels (2 Cor 4:6,7) and therefore this little lamp which once belonged to a Maccabean warrior hiding in this very cave represents to us today a believer who feels very strongly about the defilement and encroachment of idolatrous Greek thinking in the temple of the Lord, a warrior who has waged many spiritual battles contending for the faith that was handed down once for all to the saints (Jude 1:3). It has been a violent and wearying spiritual battle against your faith and it has driven you into hiding and brought you to a place where you have been buried by layer after layer of dirt, or fleshly manifestations from the hand of others and your light has been unable to shine as God intended it to. It has been so very dark around you and the attack has been so horrendous that you have felt quite unable to dig yourself out of this cave. But now, in God's impeccable timing, He is going to send help of the most unusual kind and your great worth and true identity in Christ are going to be brought to the light of day! You are going to be brought out of the cave and deposited at its mouth, almost like Jonah spat out on the beach by the whale. And guess what? It is going to be the stinky, prickly co-inhabitant of that dark cave that is going to be used to remove the layers of dirt off you and reveal your true beauty. You may even have feared the sharpness of those spines and not understand why the Lord would allow you to be buried deep in darkness in the dwelling place of such an unpleasant creature. But God has put it there to keep others away until the precise moment of unveiling. If it had not been there guarding your appointed hiding place, you would have likely been 'discovered' way too soon. In fact, that 'porcupine' has been helping to guard one of God's best kept secrets for the precise moment in history in which you are appointed to shine forth with full strength.

That little girl Hadas is seven years old and I am sure she has walked in that very area many times with her mother, but the orchestration of God ensured that she only found that lamp just before Hanukkah, the very period when it is time to fill and light lamps and celebrate deliverance from the enemy and return to consecration and holiness. You will be filled afresh and set on fire with the baptism of fire in this season. Seven is the number of completion. The trial and testing and days of darkness and pressure are complete and the work within is done. The Lord has been searching your innermost being, little lamp, and now you have been marked as a true and authentic vessel, worthy to be used as a carrier of the glory. And the day of unveiling will confirm what Heaven already knows.

Hadas was Esther's name before she entered the palace for preparation and her appointment with the king, once again a connection between Esther and Hanukkah. Her mother's name Ayelet means 'gazelle. She is the one who knew the significance and value of the lamp and what to do with it. She had understanding of the times and what to do. Her name is taken from a Hebrew phrase 'ayelethashachar' which means 'gazelle of the dawn', which is the name of the Morning Star.

2Pe 1:19   And we have the prophetic word [made] firmer still. You will do well to pay close attention to it as to a lamp shining in a dismal (squalid and dark) place, until the day breaks through [the gloom] and the Morning Star rises (comes into being) in your hearts.

The rising of the Morning Star in our hearts is a fulfilment of the coming of the dawn after a very dark night of trial, during which we have held onto the prophetic word given us. That word has been our only light in the darkness of burial. What we tend to forget is that burial with layers of earth is a necessary part of being conformed to His death. Without that hiddenness, pressure, darkness and obscurity for a measured season, the work is not complete. The 'opening' of the place where we are entombed, the appearing of the resurrection light and life of the Morning Star is only scheduled in the morning watch of our night of trial.

Hadas was Esther's original name but she received a new name which she would bear as queen – and it means 'star'! This Hanukkah, many humble little hidden lamps will be brought to light and shine like stars as they lead many to righteousness through the wisdom they carry (Daniel 12:3), even as the end-time Antiochus Epiphanies tramples some of those stars underfoot, as he wages war with the saints (Dan 8:10).

Let us look at those who receive the reward of the Morning Star and why they are found worthy to receive it:

Rev 2:24 But to the rest of you in Thyatira, who do not hold this teaching, who have not explored and known the depths of Satan, as they say--I tell you that I do not lay upon you any other [fresh] burden: Rev 2:25 Only hold fast to what you have until I come. Rev 2:26 And he who overcomes (is victorious) and who obeys My commands to the [very] end [doing the works that please Me], I will give him authority and power over the nations; Rev 2:27 And he shall rule them with a sceptre (rod) of iron, as when earthen pots are broken in pieces, and [his power over them shall be] like that which I Myself have received from My Father; Rev 2:28 And I will give him the Morning Star.

Thyatira means 'odor of affliction'. Here John describes saints who are dwelling in a place of great suffering where Jezebel (who hates the prophets) is reigning, and this crushing is releasing a perfume which ascends to the Lord and pleases Him. They have not explored the depths of satan and in spite of their weariness are holding on to the Truth they possess until Jesus comes, or manifests, as He promised, and ends the trial and testing of their worth. These are those who have continued doing the works that please Him through day after day of suffering. Yes, the assault from Jezebel has been brutal but it has been earning you a measure of authority in the spirit that you would otherwise not have been appointed, and, because you have overcome, you will be given authority to rule in wisdom and justice from the wellspring of the power of Christ within you. You will be a carrier of the Morning Star and will possess the power to bring the long night of trial to an end and open the tombs for other weary little lamps.

Ayalet is a female deer, also called a hind. The male counterpart is also known as a hart or roe. In Song of Songs 2:9, the Bride-to-be calls her Beloved 'a young hart', who is calling her to come away with Him. By Songs 8:14, they are wed and the hind and the hart will never be separated again. They move as one on the mountains of spices. In the coming season, as the baptism of fire is poured out on tried and tested earthen vessels, the Company of the Burning Hart will be released in the earth. These are they who have set Him as a seal upon their heart and upon their arm, and are burning with the fiery jealous love of the Bridegroom (Songs 8:6).

This porcupine cave was situated in the Beit Shean valley, a name which means 'House of Rest'. Beloved, did you know that the House of Rest is found in a valley, not on a mountain top? Your long season in the valley of weeping has been very necessary. It is in the valleys where deep, fertile soil is found and where great fruitfulness can come forth. A necessary part of being found worthy to enter His Rest and be a part of the House of Rest is a season dwelling in the valley:

2Th 1:4 And this is a cause of our mentioning you with pride among the churches (assemblies) of God for your steadfastness (your unflinching endurance and patience) and your firm faith in the midst of all the persecutions and crushing distresses and afflictions under which you are holding up. 2Th 1:5 This is positive proof of the just and right judgment of God to the end that you may be deemed deserving of His kingdom for the sake of which you are also suffering. 2Th 1:6 [It is a fair decision] since it is a righteous thing with God to repay with distress and affliction those who distress and afflict you, 2Th 1:7 And to [recompense] you who are so distressed and afflicted **by granting you rest** *along with us [your fellow sufferers] when the Lord Jesus is revealed from heaven with His mighty angels in a flame of fire, 2Th 1:8 To deal out retribution upon those who do not know God, and [upon those] who ignore and refuse to obey the Gospel of our Lord Jesus Christ. 2Th 1:9 Such people will pay the penalty and suffer the punishment of everlasting ruin and eternal exclusion and banishment from the presence of the Lord and from the glory of His* *power, 2Th 1:10 When He comes to be glorified in His saints, and be marvelled at and admired in all who have believed...*

Ayelet and Hadas have an interesting surname. Goldberg means 'gold mountain' but Keidar comes from a verb which means dishevelment and disarray because of grief. This verb is often used in connection with the endtimes, when the sun will grow dark and people will mourn.

Heb 12:22 But rather, you have come to Mount Zion, even to the city of the living God, the heavenly Jerusalem, and to countless multitudes of angels in festal gathering, Heb 12:23 And to the church (assembly) of the Firstborn who are registered [as citizens] in heaven, and to the God Who is Judge of all, and to the spirits of the righteous (the redeemed in heaven) who have been made perfect,

The heavenly Mount Zion and the heavenly Jerusalem, the city of gold, the Bride of the Lamb is destined to become visible during the endtimes when there is great darkness and sorrow and mourning worldwide. This is the time when you will be brought forth to arise and shine with His glory, little lamp, kept secret and hidden for such a time as this. The glory of the Morning Star will be seen upon you. Be at peace and at rest and continue to release the fragrance of your unconditional surrender to the Lord. His timing is completely perfect and He has not forgotten you! The corporate Lamp of David, the giant-slayer, will be filled and lit at Heaven's appointed moment.

Two Visions of Flaming Flight

I am always amazed at the way the Lord constantly provides information and revelation that reminds us of the end-goal while we are going through the long dark night of preparation. It imparts fresh strength to endure the process. During worship in 2012, I saw a vision unfold that was significant as we are were approaching Pentecost or Shavuot, the time when the Holy Spirit was poured out like a mighty rushing wind and manifested as flames of fire upon the heads of each one present in the upper room.

The first one I received in May 2012. During worship I saw a vision unfold that is significant considering we were approaching Pentecost when the Holy Spirit was poured out like a mighty rushing wind and manifested as flames of fire upon the heads of each one present in the upper room.

From Cocoon to Conqueror

First, I saw a small section of brilliant colour, royal blue and orange and black, almost like a peacock feather in brilliance. I was shown the section in great detail, as the Lord drew my attention to the minute feather like textures of each piece making up the patch of colors. Then my vision was pulled back enough so that I could see a single butterfly struggling out of a cocoon. I realized that the section of color I had been shown was the fine detail of a butterfly wing in extreme close-up. It was almost as if the Lord wanted me to know the infinite attention to detail that had gone into forming the smallest section of those wings.

The butterfly was struggling and exhausted as it pressed out of the narrow confines of the preparation chamber through the tiny opening into the light. It emerged with crumpled wings and sat upon a twig, spreading its wings in the light of the sun and drying out and gradually smoothed in the warmth of the sun. I was given understanding that had it tried to fly immediately upon emerging, it would have plummeted to the ground. The Spirit was emphasizing that a time of allowing the sunlight to do its part was vital in finishing the equipping of the butterfly for flight. It was imperative that it took a few moments to soak in the warmth of the sunlight; to rest in the light of the Son and allow healing of all wrinkles and crumples from birth process.

Then my vision was widened even further and I saw it wasn't only happening with one but thousands of butterflies all of the same colors; brilliant orange, deep royal blue and black. Then wind came gently at first and began to lift them up from underneath and carry them away. As they surrendered and allowed themselves to be carried, it began to blow harder and harder, finally forming a giant whirlwind full of butterflies and because of the colour of their wings, it looked like a giant swirling pillar of fire extending between heaven and earth. Then fire fell from heaven and burned the chrysalis each butterfly had emerged from. This signified there no going back, that God was burning bridges, and the only direction in which to move was forwards from now on. The purpose the chrysalis has served in providing a hidden place for the caterpillar to be completely transformed was complete and there was no more use for it.

Then the whirlwind of fiery butterflies began to move all over and touch down here and there and people were watching it in wonder. Every now and then, one person watching longingly would be sucked into the whirlwind and become part of the sweeping fiery column and as they did, fire would fall and consume the places they had come from, which looked like wooden shanties or places of poverty in some way. It was almost as if the whirlwind of fiery butterflies was reaping a harvest out of those who were hungering to be a part of what God was doing. Then the vision ended.

At church a few weeks later I saw a mini vision which was connected to this one. I saw a dark whirlwind moving back and forth. I was reminded of the vision of the butterfly whirlwind, but that was black and orange. Then one orange spark appeared in dark whirlwind and then rest of the whirlwind caught fire. I heard, "Just one spark and breath of God". "What speeds the process?" I asked the Lord. "My hands and your surrender... Only the breath of God kindles the spark to make a flame of fire." Then I saw a wooden stick being rolled between two hands, back and forth, back and forth in dry tinder to create a spark. "Don't fear the back and forth movement and rapid changes in direction with no seeming result. It will come," the Lord gently reassured me.

Ignited for Flight

The second vision concerning fiery flight was received on the morning of 12th April 2019. This morning as I was sitting quietly before Him, the Lord said to me, "Listen, daughter" and I could hear nothing but noise pollution, a kind of static. He urged me to listen more deeply and as he said this, I saw a dark grey atmosphere and peering deeply into it, I finally saw shards of what looked like diamond shaped glass strung on a piece of thread."What is it, Lord?" I asked. "It is a wind chime. Keep listening" and as I concentrated, I felt as if I was listening though a great depth of distance in the spirit. Finally, I heard a tiny sound of one piece of glass striking another. Then it happened again and again and I realised I was hearing the sound of the coming of the wind. The glass shards began to move more and more violently as the wind got closer and closer until they were tinkling incessantly.

Then I saw a mighty wind sweep through the porch of an old dilapidated house. It swept up the dead leaves that were lying around on the porch and tossed them away and then burst through the front door into a large empty hallway. As it did so, the strength of the wind knocked out some of the pieces of the staircase railing. I saw the walls of the house begin to crack at the impact of the wind's strength and wondered if it was going to fall down. "Follow the wind," the Lord instructed me and we went up those stairs to the upper floor. There was just one huge room there and the whole floor was covered with what looked like people curled up on their knees with their faces to the ground in a prayer position. They all seemed to be covered with white shrouds. There was no movement or sound in that room until the wind entered the area.

When I looked closer, I saw they were actually butterfly chrysalises. The mighty wind roared around the room touching each one and as it did so, a flame appeared on the top of each chrysalis. Then they all started rocking about as a result of something being awakened within and one by one, those within began to emerge from these chrysalises. I watched one in particular and the occupant stood on his feet in the form of a small boy and he stretched his arms in the air as a child does when it is awakened from sleep.

This boy had wings on his back and as they stretched out to form their full shape, the flame from the empty chrysalis ignited the wings and they became a set of double flames in deep orange and tipped with an almost indigo colour. They were burning but not being consumed. I looked around the room and everyone who had emerged from their own individual shroud chrysalis was also a male boy child and all had a pair of flaming wings. The mighty wind was somehow hovering gently and lovingly over the company in this upper room almost like a hen brooding over her chicks and then when the last one was completely equipped with his set of fiery flame wings, it picked up speed, sweeping them all into its movement and burst through the ceiling.

I saw the tiles of the roof being tossed every which way as the mighty wind exited the building, carrying its precious cargo of fiery flaming sons.

Then it seemed to spread out, no longer in the shape of a whirlwind but filling the whole upper atmosphere above the destroyed old house and I saw the butterflies being distributed in every direction until they were out of sight. Somehow I knew they were being carried by the wind of the Spirit to their specific appointed assignments.

Afterwards, I asked the Lord what the house represented. "It is the house of religion," He replied. "It has become an empty shell, with the souls of dead men walking littering its porch as they lie about, indolent in the sunlight. These ones are of no use to My Kingdom. My wind has come for those in the upper room; those who have submitted to the process of experiencing My death; those who have been willing to enter the tomb of transformation and be set apart for My later purposes. They have been waiting patiently in prayer for me to come and release them and now is the time. I come to set them aflame with a double portion and a baptism of fire. I come to awaken and endue with garments of fire. I come to empower and release and open up the way for their flight to their assigned places in My endtime Kingdom plans.

I will remove the ceiling with which the house of religion has hemmed them in. I come to break off the words which have bound and imprisoned and cast off and set aside my jewels. I will open up the tombs sealed by the religious spirit and no manmade barrier will hold us back any longer. We will move together, My sons of fire and I, and vacate the

premises of the place of preparation. The sky is the limit for My faithful ones. Spirit-led, Spirit-fed, flowing in a fiery anointing; the sons of the right hand are about to be released to take over their Father's business."

When I was searching for a picture of a white chrysalis, I came across this image and realized that the glass shards I saw which the Lord called a wind chime were actually the butterfly chrysalises strung on a thread. It was these sleeping ones which were being moved ever so slightly and then more strongly by the approaching wind. In other words, in spite of being totally wrapped in grave shrouds, these saints within have become super sensitive to the moving of the Spirit. Even the slightest breeze is picked up by them and the glass shards tinkling and making a sound together speaks of the fellowship of these hidden saints in the Spirit.

I then discovered that this particular chrysalis belongs to the monarch butterfly. This speaks both a negative and positive prophetic meaning. Monarch conditioning was a tool used by the CIA to control people's minds through abuse, drugs, isolation and all sorts of cruel and soul-shredding deprivation. Such is the torture of the religious spirit.

Spiritually, this connects to what the Lord said about the religious spirit speaking words over His jewels which sealed their tombs so that they would never be able to be free of the limitations and control placed on them. In my vision, I saw the Holy Spirit come in power and completely destroy the power of those schemes against His saints.

In a positive prophetic sense, the word 'monarch' means 'King', so the release of these Monarch butterflies from their tombs speaks of the release of saints with a double portion of fiery Kingly anointing. As they are carried by the wind of the Spirit to their appointed places and assignments, they will operate in a ruling anointing, passing righteous judgments by the leading of the Spirit, operating not by the sight of their natural eyes, but judging with righteousness and justice as they don't rely on their natural understanding..

For the waiting ones in the upper room, prepare to receive your double portion fiery anointing as the sons of the right hand.

7. The Coming of the Dawn of Fire

The forerunner company have been through a very long dark night of intense preparation and are now in the morning watch of their individual appointed callings. During the morning watch, light comes slowly. And what are these purified and prepared saints doing during this watch? They are worshipping:

Son 4:6   Until the day breaks and the shadows flee away, [in my thoughts] I will get to the mountain of myrrh and the hill of frankincense [to him whom my soul adores].

Myrrh is known as the oil of joy amongst the Jews, who use it to anoint a bride on her wedding day. Frankincense speaks of prayer and worship and the bread of His presence. It is a verse about intimacy between the two who adore one another. Where it says 'the day breaks', the word for 'break' in Hebrew, puach, means ' to puff, to blow, to utter, to kindle a fire'. It is a word about breath being released to do a number of things - to carry a sound and a message and to set on fire a waiting wick. The breaking of the day involves the kindling of a fire! And it is a fire that carries the sound of the voice of the One whose breath does the kindling! The messenger becomes a flame of fire whose sound brings a message.

We have spoken much about the making of messengers who are flames of fire and now we see that the kindling of that very fire occurs in the morning watch. It is in the morning watch that the perfectly prepared vessel is baptized in a fiery Word from the mouth of God as He breathes upon them and imparts of His own substance to them

The same word, puach, is translated in the following verse as 'blow'. The Bride-to-be calls upon the wind of the Spirit to breathe (blow) upon her garden (her heart) that the fragrance therein may be released for her Beloved's delight:

Son 4:16 [You have called me a garden, she said] Oh, I pray that the [cold] north wind and the [soft] south wind may blow upon my garden, that its spices may flow out [in abundance for you in whom my soul delights]. Let my beloved come into his garden and eat its choicest fruits.

So we also know that the same breath that kindles the fire also blows and releases the fragrance from within the Bride's heart. This week, I purchased an ultrasonic essential oil diffuser. This little gadget ionizes and releases aromatic and healing essential oils into the atmosphere, until the whole room is filled with fragrant oil ions, which are ministering to my body without me being even aware of them. Ultrasonic waves are acoustic (sound) energy in the form of waves which have a frequency above the human hearing range. So there are sound waves that the natural ear cannot discern, which are involved in the release of healing fragrance. In the same way, the mouth of God is releasing a sound into the waters of our earthen vessel that the natural man cannot understand or discern. These sound waves carried by His breath are causing the release of the fragrance of Christ from within us without any effort from us. We are in a state of rest, having ceased from our own fleshly labors and our hearts are still before Him, worshipping always.

Psalm 110 speaks of a company who offer themselves willingly in the day of His power. This holy army come forth in their appointed marching places in the morning watch:

Psa 110:3 Your people will offer themselves willingly in the day of Your power, in the beauty of holiness and in holy array out of the womb of the morning; to You [will spring forth] Your young men, who are as the dew.

Out of the womb of the morning' indicates a birthing which is taking place after a season of being built and prepared away from the eyes of man. It also gives us a time marker. We are brought forth quietly in the morning watch and are as the dew which falls all over the earth silently during this very time period. And more than that, we are actually a part of bringing the dawn because we are the messengers who are flames of fire; part of the corporate rising of the Sun of Righteousness. Is the sun not made up entirely of fiery flames? And each morning it rises above the horizon and brings the new day to light. In this prophetic day, the Day of the Lord, which is fast approaching, the messengers who are flames of fire carry both light and heat as they arise and shine with His glory upon them.

The fragrance of Christ with which these messengers are imbued is the essence of His character and the experience of its influence brings healing, because He is Jehovah Rapha; the Lord our Healer. Those who are being released as flames of fire also carry an anointing to heal by their very presence and the anointed words of their mouths. They form part of the coming of the Sun of Righteousness Who arises with healing in His wings.

Fiery Feather Truths

Psalm 91 speaks of being covered with His feathers:

Psa 91:4   He will cover you with His feathers, and under His wings shall you trust and find refuge; His truth is a shield and a buckler.

I have always thought of this verse as depicting us hiding from what is going on around us in terms of mayhem, but recently the Holy Spirit shed new light upon it. We are told in the 2nd part of the verse that His truth is our shield and buckler. Yet, the 1st half of the verse describes us being covered by His feathers. This tells me that His feathers represent His Truth. THIS is what shields us when all hell is breaking loose around us. The Truth of God which has carried us through our own personal dark night of the soul has shielded us from the lies sent against our minds, like a shield and buckler.

A shield is large enough to protect the whole body and is worn on the left arm where it is secured by straps. The sword of the Spirit, the Word of God is in your right hand to cause damage to the enemy. The shield is defensive and the sword is an offensive weapon. Truth both shields us and gives us power against the enemy. I have no idea why this Hebrew word 'socherah' which appears in the original language of this text was translated 'buckler', because it actually means 'to surround a person'. Therefore the verse is actually saying that His Truth both protects your whole front like a shield AND also protects your back, where you cannot see what is happening in the heat of battle. Isn't that just like the enemy to send a two-pronged attack; sending assignments toward you from the front where you can see and also launching a rear attack like a backstabber of some sort!

A buckler is a small, round, metal shield held in the hand in a "fist" grip so perhaps the circular aspect of being surrounded in the word 'socherah' caused the translators to include this kind of shield. But a buckler cannot protect your back and you must wield it yourself. The real buckler is used in battle to deflect and inflict blows on the attacker. The 'socherah' used in verse 4 gives the sense of God fighting for you and defeating the enemy in places your eyes can't detect. He has you covered!

Bridal Refuge

The reason God fights for you is because you are in covenant with Him. The word used for 'wings' in psalm 91:4 is kanaph, which also means the edge of a garment. Remember Ruth asking Boaz to spread His Wing over her. This was a reference to being brought under a marriage covenant. A marriage covenant means your enemies are His enemies, your battles are His battles and He will protect and provide for you all the days of your life. Psalm 91 is essentially a psalm for the Bride because verse 1 gives us the qualifier. - 'He who DWELLS in the secret place of the Most High shall abide under the shadow of the Almighty'. The Hebrew word for 'dwell' also means 'to settle down and marry'. This psalm cannot be quoted as superstitious protective amulet by people following their own fleshly lusts and claiming to be Believers. The protections described in these verses are part of the marriage covenant benefits of those fully surrendered to the Lamb. We can trust His marriage covenant details to be upheld by our faithful Bridegroom.

The Sun of Righteousness Who arises with healing in His wings is also a reference to the healing which is part of the marriage covenant between the Bride and the Lamb. Only those who fear the Lord have the wing of His marriage covenant truths protecting them. It has been a long dark night of preparation but the assault endured in sour souls and physical bodies is now going to be healed.

The enemy has tried his best to destroy us body and soul during the night watch, but he has been unsuccessful and everything he intended for evil will be turned for our good. The wounds of the battlefield of preparation are going to be made whole in the increasing light of this morning watch. Allow the sevenfold light of His revelation truth to penetrate your deepest being during this time. Be made completely whole, Beloved, just as Jesus emerged from the tomb on the 3rd day with the terrible scourging wounds healed.

Isa 30:26 Moreover, the light of the moon shall be as the light of the sun, and the light of the sun shall be sevenfold as the light of seven days, in the day that the LORD binds up the breach of his people and heals the stroke of their wound.

The Dawning of the Dread Champions

There have been many hazardous guesses at the interpretation of Joel chapter 2 over the years in church circles since I got saved in 1975. Most messages I have heard say that it describes a demonic army wreaking havoc. Well, I would like to suggest another view point, based on the fact that Joel 2:11 calls this mighty wave of warriors the Lord's army! Let's look at these verses with precision as I explain why I see the dread champion end-time army which has been prepared by the Lord for the day of battle that is now close at hand.

Joe 2:1 Blow the shofar in Zion; sound an alarm on My holy Mount [Zion]. Let all the inhabitants of the land tremble, for the day of the Lord is coming; it is close at hand Joe 2:2 A day of darkness and gloom, a day of clouds and of thick mists and darkness, like the morning dawn spread upon the mountains; so there comes a people numerous and mighty, the like of which has never been before and shall not be again even to the years of many generations.

There are a number of things to note about the Day of the Lord. Firstly, the sound of the shofar heralds the approach of the Day of the Lord. The shofar is a warning sound; a sound of approaching battle but also a sound of victory already assured because it is the sound of the Blood released into the spiritual atmosphere.

The coming of this army is announced by the sound of the Blood of the Lamb, the One whom they follow wherever He goes. This day that is breaking is a day of darkness, yes, but then we know from psalm 18 that darkness is His hiding place:

Psa 18:11 He made darkness His secret hiding place; as His pavilion (His canopy) round about Him were dark waters and thick clouds of the skies.

Like Joel 2:1 & 2, psalm 18 points out that both darkness and thick clouds herald the coming of the Lord. Joel 2 describes the Day of the Lord as having 3 aspects, which I will deal with one by one as they encompass a number of events in the spiritual realm:

It is a day of darkness and gloom

It is a day of clouds and thick mists

It is like the dawn spreading on the mountains.

Darkest Just Before Dawn

We must remember that in God's perspective, His day starts with evening. Genesis 1 says there was evening and morning, the first day. So we know that even in spiritual terms, when a new day begins, the darkness comes before the morning light. There are 4 watches of the night. 3 of them involve darkness. The first watch from 6-9pm contains the decrease of light and the rolling in of darkness. The fourth watch, from 3-6am involves increasing light as the sun begins to come over the horizon. There is a key given in psalm 90 which helps us to give us understanding of the times:

Psa 90:4 For a thousand years in Your eyes are as a day, yesterday, when it passes, and as a watch in the night.

We are used to hearing a day is like a thousand years, but the Word says it is also like a watch in the night. Just as there are 3 watches of darkness in a night, so we are appointed 3 days of darkness as the Day of the Lord begins. I believe this is connected to the 3&1/2 years of the rampage of the dragon in Revelation 12, during which the woman is fed and kept safe in a place prepared. The 4th watch of the night is the morning watch and it has 3 stages itself, some of which have partial darkness, adding to the other 3 dark watches and making the 3 & 1/2 days/watches/year of darkness.

Astronomical twilight

Nautical twilight

Civil twilight

Astronomical Twilight

During astronomical twilight, only those who are familiar with studying the heavens and the constellations can discern the slight increase of light. To everybody else, it looks pitch dark. This would be the time described in the saying 'it's always darkest just before dawn'. Only astronomers, those well versed in fixing their eyes on heavenly things can get their bearing from the stars at this time. The stars represent those who are wise, who are fixed in their appointed endtime positions already and are able to give light and truth in the midst of the darkness.

Nautical Twilight

During nautical twilight, one can discern shapes on the horizon but not their features. Everything is in shades of black and grey. This means one can see the outline of a man in front of you but are unable to discern whether this person is friend or foe. Some people who have journeyed with you through your night watches may have sounded like friends but when more light is given, you will discover that they have in fact been an assignment of the enemy to lead you off track. Part ways immediately!

Nautical twilight is when military attacks are usually launched on the enemy camp. Usually the enemy is sleeping and the guard who has stood watch all night is very tired and not alert. Soldiers can see enough to get their bearings and move into position quietly. This is the time when God is setting in place His mighty warriors. It is a time when you are moved by the Spirit's direction from within, but there is no sound or sight externally that exposes your positioning. People are not aware of what heaven is silently doing. It is also the time when the enemy is quietly bringing his agents of attack into your sphere. Be alert and aware, asking the Spirit to show you your enemy lying in wait for you. During nautical twilight, the horizon is clearly visible, but artificial lighting must be used to see terrestrial objects clearly.

This is a very dangerous time for the saints who have been through a night of lonely trial. Do not be tempted to switch on an artificial light if you cannot make out anything except a vague shape in front of you. There is a demonic principality called Aurora, the goddess of the dawn, who counterfeits the true light of the Sun of Righteousness. Her other name is Lilith. She is connected to militant feminism and much depravity, including sexual intimacy with humans, and will attempt to bring demonic light at this time. She will push you to take up your rightful position by force, to demand honour and recognition and your rights as the anointed of God. This is not the nature of the Lamb. We follow the Lamb wherever He leads, not the Dragon. Twilight is called 'sweet light ' by artists. Make sure you are sourcing your sweet light from the Sun of Righteousness and not the demonic goddess of the dawn. Take communion daily and decree that you receive no other light other than the true Light of the Lamb Who is the Light of the Heavenly Jerusalem. Beware of the false prophetic at this time, try to stay away from prophetic sites, because during nautical twilight, it is not yet clear if they are prophets of Baal, who have been eating at Jezebel's table or not. Rather wait in the inner chamber for light from the Spirit of Truth. The church at Thyatira (which means 'odor of affliction') are given the Morning Star if they overcome Jezebel (Rev 2:20).

Be patient. Wait for God to bring you more light from the Sun of Righteousness rising and coming towards you beyond the horizon. He may not be in full sight yet but He is sending rays of light and revelation towards you to show you what is really standing right in front of you. Wait! Do not embrace anything in front of you during this period because what vaguely looks like the shape of a friend may turn out to be an enemy when the sun rises fully. Hold your peace and wait for the entrance of His word to bring more light. God has you in a stall (Malachi 4) until the day has dawned so you can clearly discern between the righteous and the wicked!!

Nautical twilight is the time period when Ruth received her 6 measures of barley and left the threshing floor before anyone could recognize her

Rth 3:14 and she lay at his feet until the morning, but arose before one could recognize another; (nautical twilight) for he said, let it not be known that the woman came to the threshing floor. Rth 3:15 also he said, bring the mantle you are wearing and hold it. So Ruth held it, and he measured out six measures of barley and laid it on her. And she went into the town.

Civil Twilight

Civil twilight begins when the sun is 6 degrees below the horizon. The Morning star is visible during this stage of the morning watch. Civil twilight is the time when there is enough light for objects on earth to be clearly distinguished. If you can see clearly where you are positioned and what is before you, you are in the civil twilight of the morning watch and the morning star has risen in your heart. The Morning Star is the revelation of Jesus as Revelation 22:16 tells us. During the last 30 minutes of the morning watch, the morning star is visible. The Morning Star rises in our hearts, not externally on the world stage. The Kingdom of God is within us! Jesus, the Morning Star rises with revelation within us to bring the night to a complete end and to deal completely with Lilith/Jezebel/Aurora and their attack on your life.

The forerunner company, those holy to the Lord, have already been through their own personal 3 watches of darkness and are in their own 4th watch in what God is doing in their lives. For those who fear the Lord, the Sun of Righteousness is rising and bring healing, in many cases by bringing light concerning physical problems they have wrestled with all through the night, BUT for the world at large, they are standing at the brink of the rolling in of the dense darkness, 3 watches of darkness or 3 days of darkness.

The Rising of the Dark One

We see this paralleled by the 3 stages of the morning watch which the forerunners are presently in. Each stage is defined by another 6 degrees below the horizon. Astronomical twilight begins when the sun is 18 degrees below the horizon. 6 degrees later, nautical twilight begins and after a further 6 degrees of rising below the horizon, civil twilight begins. So here we have 666, the number of the name of the beast. He is darkness itself, gross darkness and he brings his own dark light. He is rising even as the dense darkness is beginning to roll in upon the earth, but he is not yet visible. He has not yet stepped onto the world stage. Just as the morning star is visible in the last 30 minutes of civil twilight, so too, the counterfeit of the real Morning Star will make His appearance within the hearts of those being led by the evil one.

Dark Without but Light Within

The last plague before the destruction of the firstborn of Egypt and the exodus of God's people from slavery or the world system was the plague of darkness. It manifested for 3 days, during which no-one in Egypt could do anything. It was a darkness that could be felt, a gross darkness so thick and evil that terror must have filled the hearts of the Egyptians. However, in the homes of God's people there was light to see by.

Exo 10:21 And the Lord said to Moses, Stretch out your hand toward the heavens, that there may be darkness over the land of Egypt, a darkness which may be felt. Exo 10:22 So Moses stretched out his hand toward the sky, and for three days a thick darkness was all over the land of Egypt. Exo 10:23 The Egyptians could not see one another, nor did anyone rise from his place for three days; but all the Israelites had natural light in their dwellings.

This was the 'gross darkness that was just before the dawn' of a new day for the Israelite slaves. After this came the transfer of Egyptian wealth to equip the people of God to build the tabernacle in the wilderness and then God drew a dividing line. He said to Moses:

Exo 12:2 This month shall be to you the beginning of months, the first month of the year to you.

Not only did He draw a line, but He changed the established calendar used by the Israelites by inserting another 1st month, and then instituted the Blood of the lamb on the doorposts and the Passover meal on the night when the Destroyer was killing the firstborn of Egypt. He struck right Pharaoh where it hurt most because his first-born son was a god-in-waiting in the Egyptians eyes. What few people know is that on the 8th of Nissan, the first-born of Egypt, who occupied the senior positions in the priesthood and government, fought a bloody battle with Pharaoh's troops, in an effort to secure the release of the Israelites and prevent the Plague of the Firstborn. This tells me that the plague of darkness so shook them that the fear of dying and even the fear of God entered their hearts and they fought to prevent any further judgments unfolding. They put all their strength into trying to get Moses' request to be fulfilled. Some Egyptians even abandoned the gods of Egypt and left with the Israelites.

In a sense, in the 3-day darkness, God was showing the Egyptians who possessed the real Light and whose revelation and belief system was really darkness. Those who were really serving the dark side experienced the fullness of what they were serving. And those who followed the God who is Light and has no darkness in Him were surrounded by the manifestation of the supernatural light of their God.

This dichotomy will be evident during the 3&1/2 years of tribulation. There will be a separation of those of the light and those of the darkness and it will be evident who belongs to each side. However, I also believe that there is coming a literal 3 days of darkness which will affect the whole earth as planet X/7X, or Niburu as some call it, passes between the earth and the sun. This planet is much bigger than the earth and its passing will take days. If you are unfamiliar with this concept, I would recommend Gill Broussard's videos on YouTube, as he has done the most comprehensive research into the

Biblical historical background for the existence of this planet and the documented effects in many ancient cultures recording the effects its passing has had on the earth.

There are also numerous believers who have been warned by the Holy Spirit that this event will indeed occur and will be preceded by strange lights filling the sky, somewhat like the Northern Lights or Aurora Borealis. It is no coincidence that the name 'Aurora' is involved because these 3 days of dense darkness will also include the mass influx of demons upon the earth. Be prepared saints of God because when the darkness for 3 days rolls in, the gravitational pull of this planet will knock out power systems worldwide. Have candles and matches and enough water and food to last 3 days in your homes. When you see the strange colors filling the whole sky, leave wherever you are and go home immediately. Cover your windows and do not open your door during those 3 days. Many demons masquerading as people in need will attempt to enter homes and there will be absolute demonic mayhem outside. Worship and pray with your family during those days and trust God to protect you. And make sure those who live in your home are aware of what to do as they see the strange sky. Notice in the following scripture how the smoke from the bottomless pit fills the atmosphere and out of that darkness come the locusts or demonic hordes:

Rev 9:1 And the fifth angel sounded, and I saw a star fall from heaven unto the earth: and to him was given the key of the bottomless pit. **Rev 9:2** *And he opened the bottomless pit; and there arose a smoke out of the pit, as the smoke of a great furnace; and the sun and the air were darkened by reason of the smoke of the pit. Rev 9:3 And there came out of the smoke locusts upon the earth: and unto them was given power, as the scorpions of the earth have power.*

Now some of you reading this are probably thinking I have lost my mind mentioning this phenomenon, but I strongly believe that it can be seen in Scripture and is part of the Lord's judgment on those who openly defy Him with their rebellion and flagrant sin. It will also be an experience which causes the undecided to turn towards Him in repentance as they are shown what the realm of darkness behaves like. This will bring in the harvest as the 3&1/2 years progresses.

Niburu's two crossings of the earth's orbit are 5 months apart, the exact amount of time that the demons released from the pit in Rev 9 are given to torment those who don't have the seal of God upon their foreheads. This called the 'first woe' in Revelation 9 and there is worse to follow. Once those demons are released during the 3 day darkness of the first Niburu crossover, they rampage on earth for 5 months until the next stage of the woes is released (Rev 9:15). It is obvious from the detail in Rev 9 that the 'rapture' has not taken place because there are still saints who have been sealed on earth as the smoke from the pit (which is the atmosphere of hell) rolls in.

The Lord also warns us to enter our chambers for a little while in Isaiah 26. Would 3 days in our chambers be 'a little while'?

Isa 26:20 Come, my people, enter your chambers and shut your doors behind you; hide yourselves for a little while until the [Lord's] indignation is passed by. Isa 26:21 For behold, the Lord is coming out of His place [heaven] to punish the inhabitants of the earth for their iniquity; the earth also will disclose the blood shed upon her and will no longer cover her slain and conceal her guilt.

In Rev 12:4, a third of the stars of Heaven are cast down by the dragon's tail, while he is waiting to devour the manchild that is coming forth. To me, this speaks of the martyrdom of saints who shine like stars during the period of the labour and birthing, and also the casting down of a 1/3 of the demonic horde in the second heaven onto the earth. This would be parallel to the release of locusts for 5 months. Then the manchild comes forth, is caught up to the throne (or receives governmental authority) and a new time period of

3&1/2 years begins, commencing with war in Heaven and the devil and his angels are cast onto the earth (verse 9). That means there are a whole lot of demonic beings running around on earth causing mayhem.

Satan goes to inhabit the son of perdition, who becomes the vessel carrying the dragon on earth, and the woman flees and is protected for and provided for in an appointed place in the wilderness. The dragon and his henchmen (demonically possessed people) are specifically making war against the saints who bear the testimony of Jesus. It is obvious that there is a Bridal company that is divinely protected during this time period, and there are others who suffer the full brunt of the demonic onslaught. Can you see in the stages of Revelation 12 how the birthing of the manchild is during the stages of the morning watch for the Bridal Company? At the same time, the level of darkness in the earth is increasing incrementally in stages.

A Wilderness Wedding

This allusion to the wilderness is a connection to the Israelite's time in the wilderness where God protected and provided for His designated bridal people. At that time in Israelite history, the wedding to God was to take place at Mount Sinai. So too, in this age, the Bridal Company will move out of the boundaries of the worldly, Babylonian Church system and journey towards the wedding in the wilderness. This is the place where she is fed and kept safe for times, time and half a time 9Rev 12).

A Day of Clouds

Joel 2 also describes the day of the Lord as a day of both clouds AND thick darkness. Now if you have ever been outside on a dark night outside the city limits, you would know that when it is very dark, you cannot see clouds overhead. So the description in Joel is not referring to natural cumulo-nimbus type clouds. Does Matt 24:30 not say that people will see Him coming or manifesting in the clouds with power and great glory?

The clouds that He is seen in are the cloud of witnesses or martyrs (the word 'marturia' means 'witness' and those who love not their lives unto death will overcome by the Blood of the Lamb and the word of their testimony).

Isaiah 19:1 describes the Lord riding in on a swift cloud to deal strongly with the idols of Egypt. So this cloud of witnesses is also carrying the righteous judgments of God into the world. Many times in the Word, God's glory appears in a cloud. So this cloud of witnesses will be carriers of the glory of God during the Day of the Lord. In Isaiah 60, there is a very interesting mention of a cloud:

Isa 60:8 Who are these who fly like a cloud, and like doves to their windows?

This is a cloud of doves and we know that the Bride in Song of Songs is referred to as a dove. His Bridal dove company will be released as witnesses during the Day of the Lord.

The cloud of witnesses are coming releasing His voice as the heavy latter rain, messengers who are coals of fire are going to be released, arrows in the hand of a Warrior

Psa 18:11 He made darkness His secret hiding place; as His pavilion (His canopy) round about Him were dark waters and thick clouds of the skies. Psa 18:12 Out of the brightness before Him there broke forth through His thick clouds hailstones and coals of fire. Psa 18:13 The Lord also thundered from the heavens, and the Most High uttered His voice, amid hailstones and coals of fire. Psa 18:14 And He sent out His arrows and scattered them; and He flashed forth lightnings and put them to rout.

These verses depict that there is light and revelation advancing before Him and His thick rain-bearing clouds release coals of fire and hailstones, speaking of the two companies of witnesses – hailstones and coals of fire.

The Rising Dawn

Then Joel 2:2 says ' *like the morning dawn spread upon the mountains; so there comes a people numerous and mighty'*. The mighty group of people are like the morning dawn is a better way of putting it. These people carry light within them. They *are* the approaching dawn because they are carriers of the light of the Sun of Righteousness. They are a Melchizedek priesthood company, both priests and kings, each carrying a measure of authority in the spiritual realm which was earned during the long dark night of preparation. This army is also described in Song of Songs:

Son 6:10 Who is she that looks forth as the dawn, fair as the moon, clear as the sun, and terrible as an army with banners?

The word translated 'looks forth' can also mean ' to be a spectacle', in other words those who gaze upon this light-bearing company are astounded at the sight of them! When an army rode forth with banners, whatever was depicted on those banners told the enemy who they represented and the authority they advanced with. The banners would strike fear into the heart of the enemy ranks!! This army of dread champions rides with the banners of all the powerful names of our God. He is Jehovah Rapha, Jehovah Shammah, Jehovah Nisi, Jehovah Shalom and many others, including the Lamb that was Slain.

Joe 2:3 A fire devours before them, and behind them a flame burns. The land is as the garden of Eden before them, and behind them a desolate wilderness. Yes, and nothing shall escape them.

This army of mighty men are surrounded by fire behind and before them. And they are headed towards Eden, having left the wilderness behind. Everyone they pass is affected by them. They change atmospheres and shake the status quo because they carry the sound of the voice of the Lord described in psalm 29. Where it is translated 'and nothing shall escape them', the Hebrew words are literally, 'yes, a remnant shall exist', which is something entirely different!! Then it goes on to describe the remnant:

Joe 2:4 Their appearance is like the appearance of horses, and like war horses and horsemen, so do they run.

Remember in Revelation, there is an army clothed in white linen riding behind the Word on His white horse as He goes forth to wage war? Here they are mentioned in Joel 2!

Joe 2:5 Like the noise of chariots on the tops of the mountains they leap--like the noise of a flame of fire devouring the stubble, like a mighty people set in battle array.

One must always look for parallel scriptures to confirm the symbolism and terms used in the Word to describe Spiritual Truth. This great army sounds like chariots riding. Isaiah 66 says that God is coming with His chariots to execute judgments and once again He is rebuking through His flames of fire; His messengers who are part of this great army described in Joel 2:

Isa 66:15 For behold, the Lord will come in fire, and His chariots will be like the stormy wind, to render His anger with fierceness, and His rebuke with flames of fire. Isa 66:16 For by fire and by His sword will the Lord execute judgment upon all flesh, and the slain of the Lord will be many.

On Yom Kippur 5779, I took a photo of a magnificent sunset and as I looked at it afterwards, the Holy Spirit opened my eyes to see a flaming lion walking and roaring and a whirlwind of fire accompanying Him. We have reached the hour in Kingdom purposes when the whirlwind of His messengers of fire will be released; sons of God led by the Spirit of God. The anointing of fire is being poured out in the morning watch of this day of the Lord. I believe in essence that Joel 2 describes the angelic armies and the army of dread warrior saints on earth working together during the Day of the Lord - a dance before two armies as Song of Songs describes the Bride (Songs 6:13). This is why Joel 2:5 says this army has a sound like chariots. It is a description of the sound of the heavenly chariots coming to wage war against all that is ungodly, working in tandem with the Bridal Company on earth.

The Birthers

Essentially, it is the translation of Joel 2:6 that has caused many to feel this chapter is about a demonic army. However I dug into the original Hebrew and it can actually be translated to say something totally different. It all depends upon the mindset of the translator as to the tone of the passage.

Joe 2:6KJV Before their face the people shall be much pained: all faces shall gather blackness.

Wrong understanding brings wrong translation. The word translated 'pained' also means 'to dance, to whirl, to bring forth, to birth, to calve' and the word translated as 'blackness' actually means ' to be illuminated, glow (from a root meaning 'to explain or make clear')'. In other words, what the Hebrew of this verse actually means is that when the people are before the face of this great army releasing His voice, they will be brought to birth, what they are carrying within will come forth and be manifested as full-term fruit, and they will dance and their faces shall glow and be illuminated i.e. They will receive the revelation and understanding needed to trigger the birthing of God's purposes for them!! This is God's army of flames of fire, carrying the sound of the very Voice that engraved and shaped them. That voice is released in power and might to bring forth life and freedom and light.

Joel 2:8 tells us that this army marches in formation and each one knows His place and does not break rank. There is no competitive spirit among these mighty warriors. Each is totally submitted to the Commander in chief as he utters His voice before His army. The

Lion of Judah is roaring and releasing His sound in waves over His army and their vessels are being filled to overflowing with the sound. It is a sound calling God's people to repentance and return amongst the release of His righteous judgments.

The Dawn upon the Mountain

This army of the Dawn is positioned and released from a mountain. There is some amazing documented historical fact concerning events on a mountain in AD66 which demonstrate what will occur concerning the temple of the Lord during these endtimes before His return. Both Josephus and a historian named Eusebius recorded that halfway through this year, the "Shekinah" Glory left the Temple and hovered over the Mount of Olives during "the siege of Jerusalem" which lasted from 66 A.D. to 70. A Jewish rabbi named Jonathan, who was an eyewitness to the destruction of Jerusalem, said the "Shekinah" Glory left the Temple and for three and a half years and "abode on the Mount of Olives, hoping that Israel would repent, but they did not; while a supernatural voice from heaven issued forth announcing, "Return, O backsliding children. Return unto Me, and I will return unto you". When they did not repent, it said, "I will return to My place" and the glory cloud lifted and disappeared from sight. 8 months after this in AD70, the temple was destroyed by the Romans.

All these events speak prophetically concerning the glory of God leaving the established church system and moving location to the mount of Olives where the ashes of the red heifer were kept for ceremonial washing for uncleanness. The voice that spoke from Heaven for 3&1/2 years brought a call to repentance, just like the two witnesses will do for the same time period. But what is interesting in these accounts is that the voice came from the Mount of Olives. Remember Zechariah saw two lampstands with a continuous supply of oil from two olive trees, and the Lord called these lampstands 'the sons of oil'. We know from Revelation that the two witnesses call fire down from Heaven and preach in a fiery manner, so these two lampstands must be lit with seven flames of fire, representing the seven lamps before the throne or the seven spirits of God. When Joel 2 speaks of the Day of the Lord being like the dawn upon the mountain, it is referring to an army of warriors carrying the fiery glory of God and releasing the sound He has filled their vessels with.

Just like in AD66 to halfway through AD69, the next 3&1/2 years will be filled with fiery messengers calling God's people to cleanse themselves of their uncleanness and all their idols and return wholeheartedly to the Lord. Elijah said, "How long will you limp between two opinions? If the Lord is God, serve Him!"

God's eyes are like a flame of fire. Where is the company that sees through His eyes, that will not judge according to the sight of their own eyes or the hearing of their own ears but with righteousness and justice will decide and decree God's judgments? They are those whose eyes are washed with tears, having experienced the broken heart of the Father as He looks upon His Jerusalem, His city that was intended to display His Name to the watching world. They are those carrying the presence of the sevenfold Holy Spirit, in the pattern of their Bridegroom, according to Isaiah 11:

Isa 11:2 And the spirit of the LORD shall rest upon him, the spirit of wisdom and understanding, the spirit of counsel and might, the spirit of knowledge and of the fear of the LORD; Isa 11:3 And shall make him of quick understanding in the fear of the LORD: and he shall not judge after the sight of his eyes, neither reprove after the hearing of his ears: Isa 11:4 But with righteousness shall he judge the poor, and reprove with equity for the meek of the earth: and he shall smite the earth (and the oppressor AMP)with the rod of his mouth, and with the breath of his lips shall he slay the wicked.

'Smite the earth and the oppressor with the rod of his mouth' – the rod of our mouth is for disciplining the flesh/earth and dealing with the enemy but there also has to be grace and compassion in dealing with those in bondage to things they cannot see. The idea is to pluck them out of the fire, hating the garment stained with sin but loving the sinner.

Remember the scene in Zechariah where Joshua the high priest stands before the throne in filthy garments? Satan stands there to accuse him but the Lord rebukes him calling Joshua a brand plucked out of the fire. He commands his filthy turban and garments to be removed and clean ones to replace them. This is the way the Father wants His church dealt with. So this company does not side with the voice of the accuser of the brethren who knows only too well how dirty Joshua's clothes are. They speak after the manner of the Lord motivated by a fiery love for the one standing before them.

Remember the manchild came forth from the midst of the Bride. He was once part of the Bridal Company and carries her DNA, but also that of his Father. The manchild is raised to a ruling and reigning position and the Bride who has produced him from her midst and her travail is set apart in a place of protection and feeding. The manchild is a son; a corporate Company of the Sons of God who have been raised to rulership at the right hand. I believe it is the manchild Company who are tasking with feeding and protecting the Bride during these 3&1/2 years, operating in both the rod of judgment and the staff of a shepherd, teaching and providing safe pasture for the Bride, the Lord's ewe lamb. They form part of the rising of the Sun of Righteousness and the truths they carry bring healing to the Bride.

Isa 60:1 Arise, shine; for thy light is come, and the glory of the LORD is risen upon thee. Isa 60:2 For, behold, the darkness shall cover the earth, and gross darkness the people: but the LORD shall arise upon thee, and his glory shall be seen upon thee. Isa 60:3 And the Gentiles shall come to thy light, and kings to the brightness of thy rising.

This chapter is addressed to Zion and the word 'light' in verse 1 is 'or' which also means 'the dawn'. Arise and release your light for your dawn has come and the glory of the Lord has arrived. But who brings it in? The sons of God who carry the glory; who ARE the Dawn spread upon the mountains, they bring the glory and pour it out in the midst of His people. Earthly Zion is the place where the House of David was situated and heavenly mount Zion is where the church of the Firstborn are gathering. It is where the heavenly Jerusalem is situated (Heb 12:22). Further on in this passage, the prophet says that flocks of Kedar shall be gathered to Zion. Who are these sheep that are arriving?

Isa 60:7 All the flocks of Kedar shall be gathered together unto thee, the rams of Nebaioth shall minister unto thee: they shall come up with acceptance on mine altar, and I will glorify the house of my glory.

Kedar means 'dusky, dark' and the Bride in Song of Songs chapter 1:5 describes herself as being dark like the tents of Kedar. So we know the flocks that come for feeding are the Bridal flock, the very flock which the Great Shepherd leads out. And we see it is the RAMS that minister. Nebaioth means 'fruitfulness' and a ram is a mature male sheep - a son. So the fruitful sons of God will be ministering and feeding the Bridal sheep on Mount Zion, where the church of the Firstborn are gathering. The firstborn receives a double portion, so here those that minster have the double portion anointing of Elijah.

Isa 60:8 Who are these that fly as a cloud, and as the doves to their windows?

The manchild company are the ones who fly as a cloud of witnesses and release the Bide who is called a dove by the Bridegroom in Song of Songs, to fly to her appointed window. This window is a reference to the windows of Heaven which are opened to release a blessing Malachi 3:10. The manchild teaching releases the Bride into the fullness of her inheritance. Interestingly, the Hebrew word for 'window' also means 'dovecote', which is a home or place of rest for the dove. The Bridal dove's resting place is in heavenly places, far above the turmoil unfolding on earth, and the teaching and feeding of the manchild company release her to find rest in this heavenly place. From this place of dwelling, she also can pour out of the riches of the meat contained in the storehouses of heaven. When the windows of Heaven are opened, the Lord also rebukes the devourer so your seed and your fruit cannot be stolen any longer - no more miscarriage of His purposes through your life; no more full-term abortions! (Mal 3:11). The woman is kept safe and fed in the wilderness for 3 & 1/2 years through this manchild company and the angelic army which works with them.

A Sign from the Ashes

On November 29th 2016, a man named Isaac discovered a burned Bible page from the book of Joel at Dollywood in Pigeon Forge, TN, in USA. The final verse on the page was Joel 2:1 about the Day of the Lord. Of all the pages that could have been spared in the fire, Almighty God organised for these ash-covered verses to be left as a message and a warning. The fact that it appeared when a fire raged through Dollywood, a family-themed amusement park owned by professing Christian, Dolly Parton, is an indication that cleansing and refining fire is appointed the entertainment industry which has permeated the Church system which professes to follow the teaching of Jesus Christ. The day of the Lord is at hand. We are now 2&1/2 years from the day that page was unearthed from the ashes and I strongly believe we are watching the beginnings of the Day of the Lord unfold.

River of Fire

During 2008, I had a very strong visitation of the Spirit and a word of prophesy came forward which has yet to be fulfilled: 'I, the Lord, will dwell in the midst of My people and I shall be a wall of fire round about her and I shall be the glory in the midst of her, for

I have come on the throne of My glory with My many angels and I am separating the sheep from the goats, says the Lord, and for those who are the sheep, who have followed My voice and who know Me, I say to you, inherit the kingdom that was prepared for you from before the foundation of the world, for behold the heavenly city is descending out of heaven and it is surrounded by a wall and that wall is the wall of fire and that wall is My bride and that wall are My messengers of fire and that wall are those who have laid down their lives, the vessels of gold that have laid down their lives and have said Lord we will go where You go and where You stay, we will stay and our lives are Yours and we surrender to You.

Therefore thus says the Lord, I shall come with My chariots of fire and I shall come with My stormy wind and I shall shake the earth and My hand of favour shall be seen to be toward My servants and My hand shall be seen against My enemies, for I am coming with fire to judge the whole earth, says the Lord. And the fire of My Spirit shall burn within the bones of My people and the fire of My Spirit shall burn and surround My church and I will protect her and I will be a wall of fire round about her, even as a fire wall protects your computer from viruses, thus says the Lord, I will be a wall of fire around My church and no unclean thing shall anymore enter in there, for as any unclean thing tries to enter in, it shall be judged by the fire, but I say there is a highway of holiness and no unclean thing shall walk there, but My bride shall be found there, My bride shall be found walking with the fire of the Holy Spirit and the power of the Holy Spirit and the gifts of the seven fold Holy Spirit, for I shall be unto her a river flowing in this day, says the Lord.'

the sight of the glory of the Lord
was like devouring fire
on the top of the mountain
Exodus 24:17

8. The Golden Altar

The contents of the incense, whose fragrance is being released by fire at the golden altar, contain much prophetic significance. In John's vision, he saw that this incense played a pivotal role in end time events. Once it had been ignited and cast on the earth, there was an outbreak of heavenly sounds in the earth:

Rev 8:3 And another angel came and stood over the altar. He had a golden censer, and he was given very much incense (fragrant spices and gums which exhale perfume when burned), that he might mingle it with the prayers of all the people of God (the saints) upon the golden altar before the throne. Rev 8:4 And the smoke of the incense (the perfume) arose in the presence of God, with the prayers of the people of God (the saints), from the hand of the angel. Rev 8:5 So the angel took the censer and filled it with fire from the altar and cast it upon the earth. Then there followed peals of thunder and loud rumblings and blasts and noises, and flashes of lightning and an earthquake.

This golden altar is before the throne of God and the fragrance of the prayers of His people is always rising before Him as a pleasant odour. However a time comes when the golden censer comes into play and casts a measured portion of fiery, fragrant incense upon the earth and the result is earth shattering – literally! The word translated 'thunderings' actually means 'roar'! So the fusing of fiery coals with the incense releases the roar of God through these coals of fire - and the result is light and revelation, 'noises' or 'sayings' and an earthquake. When people know the Truth, it sets them free. Therefore, this release of light and revelation will trigger a release of captives, who have been held prisoner for a long time by the lies they have erroneously embraced, thinking they are the truth. Prison cells will be shaken by the earthquake that follows the release of this roar through the coals of fire. Answers to long seasons of intercession for bound loved ones will suddenly be manifested in the earth realm and breakthrough will occur all over the earth.

The earthly version of this golden censer was used on the holiest day of the year, Yom Kippur, when the high priest entered the Holy of Holies to make intercession for the people.

Lev 16:12 And he shall take a censer full of coals of fire from off the altar before the LORD, and his hands full of sweet incense beaten small, and bring it within the veil. Lev 16:13 And he shall put the incense upon the fire before the LORD, that the cloud of the incense may cover the ark-cover that is upon the testimony, that he die not.

There are saints, who, like Anna of old, remain at this golden altar, their whole lives being one of prayer and fasting and worship before the Lord. Others come and go, in between their involvement in the things of the world, but for those who have doves' eyes, their focus is upon the throne of God and their hearts continually worship Him in this position. The position of the golden altar before the curtain and the incense which is burned thereon, day and night, is a picture of those whose lives are a continual fragrance released by the fire of their love for Him.

However, we are also told there are two handfuls of incense, which has been crushed finer than the rest, which is taken in the cupped hands of the high priest into the Holy of Holies to create a fragrant cloud before the ark of His presence. There are a portion of saints appointed extra crushings and temperings, and it may seem unfair when you look around you at others who do not experience such intense breakings. Yet there is purpose.

You are appointed to be carried beyond the point where other intercessors live, right before the ark of His manifest presence, to be set ablaze and form part of the fragrant cloud impregnated with His presence; this cloud of witnesses who emit the powerful fragrance of Christ from their lives, as the fire of God burns constantly within them.

These ones dwell with the everlasting burnings, having lingered much in the presence of the mercy seat.

Yom Kippur was also the day the Jubilee shofar was blown, announcing freedom from slavery. When this happened, every slave was to be returned to his family and to his ancestral possession. Loved ones who had been slaves for many years were suddenly released by the sound of this shofar blast and were soon reunited with their families!

Rev 8:5 So the angel took the censer and filled it with fire from the altar and cast it upon the earth. Then there followed peals of thunder and loud rumblings and blasts and noises, and flashes of lightning and an earthquake.

The word 'cast' can also be translated 'sent'. Here is depicted a thrusting forth of fragrant, fire-filled harvesters into the harvest field. Like Anna who rushed out to tell everyone she saw about the Messiah, so too, these fiery zealous coals are thrust into the earth realm, sent on Heaven's missions; bringing the harvest to completion. These coals are poured out with a heavy coating of incense, which is consumed by the fiery heat coming from the coals and turned into a perfumed, smoking cloud as it hits the earth realm.

And from this cloud comes a sound, a Royal roar that shatters prison bars and sets the captive free! Just like the bridal palanquin of Solomon (Songs 3:7-11) carrying the happy royal couple, surrounded by 60 mighty men, emerged from the wilderness with pillars of fragrant smoke, so too this outpouring upon the earth is a united, fragrant outpouring of the Bride and the Groom who have become one, and go forth to administer His righteous judgments in the earth.

Isa 66:15 For behold, the Lord will come in fire, and His chariots will be like the stormy wind, to render His anger with fierceness, and His rebuke with flames of fire.

Carriers of His Fragrance

What is seen in Revelation 8 is the answer to the centuries of intercession of the saints. The bowls are full and it is time to pour out the answer in the form of a release of messengers of fire on the earth, who carry the fragrance which is acceptable to the Father. So let us look deeper into the ingredients of this incense named in Exodus.

Exo 30:34 Then the Lord said to Moses, Take sweet spices--stacte, onycha, and galbanum, sweet spices with pure frankincense, an equal amount of each-- Exo 30:35 And make of them incense, a perfume after the perfumer's art, seasoned with salt and mixed, pure and sacred.

The Holy Spirit is the Apothecary or Perfumer, creating within us the required recipe for dwelling at this altar of gold. The word 'perfume' in Hebrew means 'to fumigate' and comes from a root word meaning 'to turn into fragrance by fire, to drive out occupants'. This incense is tempered or pulverised with crystals of salt. Salt is a preservative which eradicates any form of decay. In other words, salt drives back the operation of death. It represents Truth, which purifies, disinfects and drives out any demonic occupant. Those whose lives embody this perfume are carriers of an anointing of yoke breaking Truth which drives back the hold of death in any form. The fiery Truth of God will test every man's work, whether it be of Life or Death. He is coming as a Refiner's Fire to the Church and He is salting us with fiery Truth in order to preserve us when the Destroyer passes overhead.

Mar 9:49 For everyone shall be salted with fire.

A Salt Covenant is an eternal, unbreakable covenant, so the addition of salt and fire to the incense ingredients for the golden altar gives it a sense of an eternal, unbreakable covenant being forged with these ones residing here.

Onycha

Onycha means 'to peel off by a concussion of sound', and comes from a root word meaning 'to roar'. Onycha burns blue when exposed to fire. Onycha is the roar that comes from your life, peeling off layers that hold people captive by a concussion of sound. You shake atmospheres by your presence. The fragrance of Christ in you contains a roar that opens prison doors, so step into the darkness with confidence in Him Who utters His voice and releases His royal roar through your yielded vessel. ...But what of the contribution of the other ingredients to the fragrance?

Stacte

Stacte is clear, reddish myrrh which exudes spontaneously from the tree, or which is released when lumps of myrrh are bruised. In other words, stacte is offered freely. Myrrh is harvested by making slashes on the tree bark. Therefore the harvesting of myrrh is a result of interference by the hand of man; whereas stacte is a freewill offering. Myrrh was released into the spiritual atmosphere when Jesus was whipped with the cat of nine tails by the Roman soldier. Yet, because He offered Himself willingly, stacte was also released as He was bruised for our iniquities. God's people will also offer themselves willingly in the day of His power. They will say, "Here am I, Lord. Send me!"

The Hebrew word for 'stacte' comes from a root word meaning 'to speak by inspiration, to prophesy'. When fully surrendered to the Bridegroom, the testimony of Jesus which is the spirit of prophecy just oozes from you without any effort. You speak by inspiration of the Spirit of Truth. What is even more powerful is the fact that your life speaks or releases a sound that carries spiritual authority. You are conformed to His death by living in a posture of 'Not my will, but Yours be done' and so the life, power and fragrance of Christ flows from you.

Galbanum

Galbanum is a golden yellow colour and burns with a purple flame. The word 'galbanum' means 'fat, the richest, finest, choice part'. Do you remember Mary chose the 'choice part' which was sitting at His feet, drinking in the words that came from the lips of Jesus? Those who have chosen the choice part are His choice ones:

Son 6:9 But my dove, my undefiled and perfect one, stands alone [above them all]; she is the only one of her mother, she is the choice one of her who bore her. The daughters saw her and called her blessed and happy, yes, the queens and the concubines, and they praised her.

We would say, "She is the cream of the crop; the one of the highest quality". The Hebrew word 'choice' used here means 'beloved, pure, empty'. It comes from a root word meaning 'to clarify, cleanse, purge and polish, to select'. Here we have the whole refining process in a nutshell, and those who exude galbanum have cooperated with the trying, refining process and have been selected for their high quality. This dove company stands alone, above the rest in purity and clarity of heart. They are those who can dwell with the everlasting burnings and when the fire consumes them, they display the royal colour of purple, signifying they are of the King's household.

Frankincense

Frankincense was used with every offering in the temple, except the sin and jealousy offerings. Therefore its presence on the altar of incense signifies that the work of cleansing from sin is complete - and also that no test for adultery needs to be conducted here. This company is faithful and has undivided hearts. The dove of the Bridegroom is undefiled, meaning 'complete, without blemish'. Frankincense burns white and comes from the root word for 'heart'. The white flame signifies a pure heart and we know that the pure in heart shall see God (Matt 5:8). Notice that it is the pure 'in heart' that are described i.e. The fragrance and flame of Frankincense is burning. The Lord said to me that one is only qualified to wear frankincense when myrrh has done its deep cleansing work and your heart is declared undivided. When you have made your journey through the wilderness of preparation successfully, then frankincense and all the sweet spices come forth from our hearts as a fragrant preparation for intimacy after the wedding ceremony. If the burning incense could speak English, it would be a wholehearted "Yes, I do" to the Father's question, "Who takes this Man as her lawful, wedded Husband?"

Frankincense is the fragrance of the open tomb, the fragrance of life from the dead and of surrender. Only when one's heart is fully Christ's, the fragrance of frankincense begins to be emitted. The expertly crafted perfume of frankincense and other 3 sweet spices combined in the incense recipe speak of marriage and becoming one in a salt covenant, before entering the Holy of Holies with Bridegroom; our High Priest after the order of Melchizedek.

A Bride after My own Heart

When I was looking at the incense and its characteristics, the Holy Spirit pointed out something amazing. We know that as we behold Him, we are changed from glory to glory and that 1 Corinthians says that when we see Him, we shall be like Him. Well, right here in this burning incense is a visual demonstration of the Bride becoming a mirror image of her Groom, bone of His bone and flesh of His spiritual flesh. Let me explain...

God gave instructions to Moses on the mountain about the making of the breastplate for the High Priest; and He was very specific about the colors that must be used:

Exo 28:15 You shall make a breastplate of judgment, in skilled work; like the workmanship of the ephod shall you make it, of gold, blue, purple, and scarlet [stuff], and of fine twined linen.

Threads of four different colors were interwoven with fine white linen to form the foundation upon which the twelve gemstones representing the twelve tribes of Israel would be set in gold settings. Not coincidentally, these four colors, plus white, are found in the characteristics of the incense burning on the golden altar:

Gold – galbanum in its solid form

Blue – onycha as it burns

Purple – Galbanum's flame colour

Scarlet – Stacte's color

White – Frankincense's flame colour.

So when Bride's heart is set aflame and burns with fiery zeal, these jewel colors are seen and it is clearly displayed that she has the heart of the Bridegroom and is recognized as bone of his bone and flesh of his flesh, one worthy to be the Bride of the Lamb. She has the same heart for His people that He has and carries His heartbeat for all the nations of the earth.

The blended fragrance released by these spices expertly blended together as a sacred perfume move the heart of the Bridegroom. We can see a demonstration of the release of God's righteous judgments accompanied by the very colors of the flames of the incense depicted in the book of Esther. After Esther had won the heart of the Bridegroom King with her banquet of love, she again approached the king and received permission, along with Mordecai the faithful intercessor at the gate, to craft a decree counteracting what the enemy wanted to do in destroying her people. When Mordecai rode out of the palace to announce this decree, he was clothed in the colors of the flames from the altar of incense!

Est 8:15   And Mordecai went forth from the presence of the king in royal apparel of blue and white, with a great crown of gold and with a robe of fine linen and purple; and the city of Shushan shouted and rejoiced.

Mordecai wore blue and white, gold and purple. All are colors released at the altar of incense. The faithful intercessors at the altar of incense are raised to honour, just as Mordecai was. Note that he came forth from the presence of the king! Those who have poured out their lives at the altar of incense in prayer and worship come forth from the presence of the King with a fiery anointing, releasing His righteous judgments.

When God's righteous judgments go forth, they are not something to be feared if you are walking in the fear of the Lord. They bring recompense upon the enemy and all he has come up with to destroy you! Those who dwell at the altar of incense play a part in releasing His righteous judgments in the earth. This is why there are thunderings, voices and an earthquake when the censor of fiery coals is cast upon the earth! And those who dwell in the city where the King resides, experience great rejoicing because He is decreeing recompense upon their enemies.

For those who have been purged and purified by the spirit of judgment and burning and now find themselves safely anchored on Mount Zion, there will be green pastures and still waters and, more importantly in these difficult days ahead, divine protection and illumination. The flaming fire of the Lord is found in Zion, to provide light in the darkest night:

Isa 31:9 ...says the Lord, Whose fire is in Zion and Whose furnace is in Jerusalem.

God has a furnace in Jerusalem and the fire that heats it is found in Zion. Those are two different areas; Mount Zion is a portion of the whole geographical area of Jerusalem. Jerusalem is the container which holds the fiery coals. It is not on fire itself. In the natural Jerusalem, mount Zion is the place where the city of David is located and where King David had his palace. It is in this place, where those of the house of David are anchored, that the everlasting burnings are situated, described in Isaiah 33. The Bridal company are dwelling in the palace with the Bridegroom, not in the rest of the city. They are set-apart for the King. They are also set on fire as burning coals.

Measured and Released to Rule

In Revelation 11, John is informed that the temple and the altar and those who worship therein are exempt from the trampling that occurs for three and a half years.

Rev 11:1 A REED [as a measuring rod] was then given to me, [shaped] like a staff, and I was told: Rise up and measure the sanctuary of God and the altar [of incense], and [number] those who worship there. Rev 11:2 But leave out of your measuring the court outside the sanctuary of God; omit that, for it is given over to the Gentiles (the nations), and they will trample the holy city underfoot for 42 months (three and one-half years).

The word translated 'gentiles' actually refers to those who do not serve the One True God and are therefore pagan. Beloved, the altar of incense is the place to be found in the days we are entering into.

John, the Beloved, was given a reed like a rod to measure the sanctuary and the altar of incense and record those who worship there (Rev 11:1). The Hebrew word for 'rod' also means 'a scepter or staff; a stick for fighting, writing or ruling'. It is from the centre of Zion that the scepter of God is extended to rule in the midst of our enemies, according to psalm 110. So those who are getting ready to launch in perfect alignment with Heaven will be releasing decrees and books and sounds that cause massive change in the earth and bring alignment with the Kingdom of Heaven in their chosen areas of influence. They will be led by surrendered hearts and not by their own understanding; providing a breathtaking display of perfect oneness with their Creator for those who observe them. Fiery coals accompany the moving of God's feet as He comes to judge the earth and deal with the powers of darkness through His fiery messengers. They have been set alight by the words of His mouth:

Psa 18:8 There went up smoke from His nostrils; and lightning out of His mouth devoured; coals were kindled by it.

2Sa 22:12 He made darkness His canopy around Him, gathering of waters, thick clouds of the skies. 2Sa 22:13 Out of the brightness before Him coals of fire flamed forth.

The burning coals accompany the living creatures as the glory of God arrives on the scene:

Eze 1:13 In the midst of the living creatures there was what looked like burning coals of fire, like torches moving to and fro among the living creatures; the fire was bright and out of the fire went forth lightning.

The burning coals on the altar are those who have, like the swallow, made their nest or dwelling place at the altar of God, as psalm 84 describes. As I have mentioned earlier, the golden altar is the altar of incense just in front of the veil, and it is from this place that an angel takes coals and adds much incense and casts it on the earth, releasing an outbreak of Heavenly power and sound:

Rev 8:3 And another angel came and stood over the altar. He had a golden censer, and he was given very much incense (fragrant spices and gums which exhale perfume when burned), that he might mingle it with the prayers of all the people of God (the saints) upon the golden altar before the throne. Rev 8:4 And the smoke of the incense (the perfume) arose in the presence of God, with the prayers of the people of God (the saints), from the hand of the angel. Rev 8:5 So the angel took the censer and filled it with fire from the altar and cast it upon the earth. Then there followed peals of thunder and loud rumblings and blasts and noises, and flashes of lightning and an earthquake.

There will be a release of heavenly sounds, revelation and the voice of God resounding through these perfectly aligned vessels, released as burning coals of fire from the censor to minister a message that shakes the earth. They usher in the sounding of the seven trumpets.

Copycat Colors, Counterfeit Coals

Baal or Bel (from which they get Beltaine, the ancient pagan festival celebrated on May 1st) is the pagan god of fire and just as God is preparing messengers who are flames of fire, the captain of the host of dark angels is grooming his diabolical messengers, pungent with the sulphurous flames of hell. In a similar display of the counterfeit, we see that the woman who rides the beast also displays some of the colors of the holy incense:

Rev 17:4 The woman was robed in purple and scarlet and bedecked with gold, precious stones, and pearls, [and she was] holding in her hand a golden cup full of the accursed offenses and the filth of her lewdness and vice.

Note, however, that there is no blue displayed. It takes the hottest part of the flame, a blue flame to turn the incense into fragrance by fire. The fire is not intended to warm the toes of the bride, but to set her aflame with a cleansing fire. Therefore this harlot bride has not subjected herself to the Refiner's fire. She tries to rule and dispense wine without the fiery seal of God's approval and is without purity of heart. Therefore she offers abominations and filth in the cup she holds out. Blue is also the colour of heavenly revelation, of which she dispenses none!

The locusts released from the abyss in Revelation 9 also represent the counterfeit bridal company, moving in demonic power. They have faces of people (in other words, these are people possessed by demons) and breastplates of iron and something 'like' golden crowns. They have teeth like lion's, but there is no roar of the Lion of the tribe of Judah from their spirits! They are also accompanied by smoke, but it is black as opposed to the smoke of the altar of incense which is white and blue and purple. And there is no salt of any kind present – Truth is absent and Abbadon is at their head.

Rev 9:2 He opened the long shaft of the Abyss (the bottomless pit), and smoke like the smoke of a huge furnace puffed out of the long shaft, so that the sun and the atmosphere were darkened by the smoke from the long shaft. Rev 9:3 Then out of the smoke locusts came forth on the earth, and such power was granted them as the power the earth's scorpions have. ... Rev 9:7 The locusts resembled horses equipped for battle. On their heads was something like golden crowns. Their faces resembled the faces of people. [Joel 2:4.] Rev 9:8 They had hair like the hair of women, and their teeth were like lions' teeth. Rev 9:9 Their breastplates (scales) resembled breastplates made of iron, Rev 9:11 Over them as king they have the angel of the Abyss (of the bottomless pit). In Hebrew his name is Abaddon [destruction], but in Greek he is called Apollyon [destroyer].

One Corporate Holy Sound

Once these five months of torment inflicted on all those who do not bear the Lord's seal is past, a very interesting thing happens:

Rev 9:13 Then the sixth angel blew [his] trumpet, and from the four horns of the golden altar which stands before God I heard a solitary voice

There is a voice or sound released from the very place that the incense is burning on the golden altar. This word translated 'solitary' is a feminine word meaning 'a' or 'one'. So there is a sound which comes forth after the sixth trumpet. It is one sound, a single or united sound, not many different sounds and its purpose is to issue a decree to release the judgments held back for this particular moment in world history. These judgments are carried out with the intention of bringing the remaining two thirds of mankind to repentance as Rev 9:20,21 indicates. However, even though a third of men perish, the hardness of people's hearts prevents them turning from their sorcery, murder, idolatry and thefts.

It seems to me that it is those who are sealed before the locusts are released, which are those found at the golden altar, worshipping and praying before the throne. They are dwelling in unity and are in one accord in one place before the throne and from them a united sound is released, triggering the executing the judgments written.

Look at how the Bride is described emerging from the wilderness on the day of her wedding:

Son 3:6 Who or what is this [she asked] that comes gliding out of the wilderness like stately pillars of smoke perfumed with myrrh, frankincense, and all the fragrant powders of the merchant?

The Hebrew word used here for 'perfumed' means 'to turn into fragrance by fire, to fumigate and drive out previous occupants'. That is a powerful approaching Company which causes the darkness to flee before it! The burning coal fragrant Bride is also described as a company of mighty men, well equipped to deal with the enemy:

Son 3:8 They all handle the sword and are expert in war; every man has his sword upon his thigh, that fear be not excited in the night.

The mighty men are those whose lives have been laying in complete surrender upon the altar of God until they have become coals of fire, consumed with the fiery zeal of the Lord of Hosts. Then they are released and cast on the earth, speaking the words of God and releasing the revelation of Heaven which causes the earth to shake and the judgments written to be executed!

End-Time Fiery Judgments begin

The fire which broke out in the roof of the Notre Dame Cathedral on April 14th 2019 is a powerful prophetic sign of God's coming judgment on all paganism and idolatry that is cloaked in religious sounding phrases and done in His Name. The cathedral is dedicated to the Virgin Mary; a veiled allusion to the Queen of Heaven and connected to worship of Semiramus and Nimrod. Covered in demonic statues and pagan imagery mixed in with statues of saints, it is situated right at the geographical centre of Paris, the city of Lights. What a counterfeit of the Church of Jesus Christ who is supposed to be the light of the world.

The original ground was home to a pagan temple dedicated to Jupiter who is the supreme Roman god and the edifice has a history of the blood of the saints spilled within its walls. During the French Revolution, it was rededicated and called 'The Temple of reason', an atheistic group that denied the existence of Yahweh God. Then it was taken over and renamed by the Cult of the Supreme Being, who refused to acknowledge that there was only one God, but in actual fact were worshipping satan as the supreme being.

The Flame Kindler

It is most interesting that there is no known cause for the fire. I believe God Almighty kindled that flame:

Jer 43:12 And I will kindle a fire in the temples of the gods of Egypt;

Of course, just as in the case of the destruction of the twin towers on 9/11, it has been declared that they will rebuild this cathedral better than before. Religion lifts its fist in the face of God and decrees that He will not stop their idolatry. Well, we will see... The end of the Book tells a different story!

A cathedral spire generally marks the building as a place of Christian worship and the fact that this was consumed by fire and thrown down declares that this edifice is not a place where the Spirit of the Living God is to be communed with. In fact, on top of this spire was a rooster containing 3 relics; a piece of the crown of thorns and bits of two patron saints of Paris. In the 9th century, Pope Nicholas made the rooster official. His decree was that all churches must display the rooster on their steeples or domes as a symbol of Peter's betrayal of Jesus. Well, that says it all...

Now the judgment of God is coming on that which is done in His Name but actually being in reality a total betrayal of Jesus. As the fire raged, people were on their knees on the pavement singing 'Ave Maria', not crying out to God Himself for mercy but singing to the Queen of Heaven. How tragic the blindness of the deceived sheep is.

A Window of Opportunity to Flee

At the beginning of April 2019, I had a vision which I feel is connected to this fiery sign in France. Not only does it involve fire and the whirlwind of the Lord but a removal of the roof of the House of Religion so that His messengers of fire can be set free. This vision is shared in depth in the chapter 'Set on Fire as the Darkness Falls'. I titled it 'Ignited for Flight' and of course, flight is both soaring in the heavens led by the Spirit of God and also the flight from the flood of the Dragon. Some of the worst persecution of Believers has been done in history by the Catholic Church. The blood of many saints on upon their hands as they persecuted all who would not come under the skirts of Rome. And in these end-times, once again there is an Endeavour to gather all sectors of the Church under these skirts; both denominational and charismatic leaders have bowed their knee to the present pope and desecrated the memory of all those true Believers who gave their lives for their faith over the centuries. As the New World Order arises, the One World religion will again, in the name of God, pursue and persecute all who would follow the Lamb whenever He goes and believe that only the Blood of Jesus saves and delivers. How interesting that just before this fire broke out, the statues of the 12 apostles and four evangelists were removed for cleaning AND for some unfathomable reason (other that it

being a prophetic sign), their heads were removed as they did so. The One World Religion will martyr many of the sent ones after they complete their assignments.

The open ceiling of the burnt Notre Dame Cathedral to me speaks of a window of escape for the dove company who have been held captive within the cage of Religion. "Come Out of Her and Be separate!" says the Lord of Hosts, "So that you do not share in her plagues." Remember, precious set-apart ones, when the fires of judgment begin to topple the spires of established Churchianity, there will be a window of opportunity to flee the wrath of the dragon. Don't hesitate or look behind like Lot's wife, but run to the feast prepared for you in the wilderness. You will be kept safe there.

Flashing Coals and Thunderbolts

The word Judge (Shepat) is extremely forceful, beginning with the letter Shin (which represents the fire of God), followed by the bursting/breaking letter Peh and ending with the sharp biting letter Tet. Peh is the letter symbolizing the breath of God. So we see that fiery judgments are released from the lips of the Judge of the whole earth. The word translated 'burning coals' is 'reseph', also meaning 'arrow, lightening, thunderbolt'.

Psa 18:13 The LORD also thundered in the heavens, and the Highest uttered His voice; hail stones and coals of fire.

The sound of His voice transports hailstones and coals of fire forth in judgment. WE see a fiery judgment described in Ezekiel 10:

Eze 10:2 And [the Lord] spoke to the man clothed in linen and said, Go in among the whirling wheels under the cherubim; **fill your hands both hands with coals of fire from between the cherubim and scatter them over the city**. And he went in before my eyes.

Do you remember how two handfuls of incense went into the Holy of Holies, carried in the cupped hands of the High Priest? Now two handfuls of coals of fire go out to be scattered as judgment is carried out over the city.

Eze 10:7 And a cherub stretched forth his hand from between the cherubim to the fire that was between the cherubim, and took some of it and **put it into the hands of the man clothed in linen**, who took it and went out.

The man in linen has just sealed those who weep at mercy seat. They are the coals of fire who stand at the threshold and intercede for their unfaithful brethren, and the glory comes upon them to equip them as they go forth to their various assignments in the city.

Cleansing and Releasing the Saints

Do you remember when Isaiah saw the Lord high and lifted up and His train filling the temple? At this point, the prophet realized he had unclean lips and dwelt among a people who also had unclean lips. Then a live coal was taken from off the altar to cleanse him.

There will be many burning coals sent to teach the people the difference between the holy and the profane; to cleanse the people whom God has assignments for. After Isaiah was cleansed, he received his prophetic assignment and could fulfill it, even though surrounded by those of unclean lips. He was a vessel made holy by a burning coal from the altar.

One thing about a fiery coal - it can set others on fire! Those who are able to not only dwell with the everlasting burnings but become vessels carrying the fire of God are able to be used to ignite other flames of fire. Just like the central candle on the menorah (called the shamash or servant lamp or candlestick) is lit first and then used to light the other 6 lamps, so too the servant company of His set-apart sons will be used to kindle a fire in the earth; to set alight the rest of the Bridal Company.

The other six lamps are full of oil but they lack the flame of fire which will complete the process.

The shamash sons must move as a forerunner fiery company and set the bride aflame. The sons of God and the Bride will both carry fiery anointings, truly becoming a city set upon a hill, Mount Zion, and functioning as the Light of the World during the time of dense darkness that covers the earth.